From our mother tongues to the
letter of the law, our lives are made
of language. Words write our world;
they are the elementary particles
of social relations. We can't escape
their dominion, but we can play
with them, we can subvert them,
turning them against the forces that
would fix us alongside them in a
matrix of control. There is a war
within every word, and this little
lexicon is a legion rising in mutiny.

Contradictionary

a bestiary *of* words *in* revolt

CRIMETHINC. WRITERS' BLOC | SALEM, OR | 2013

This book is available for $8 + shipping from

CrimethInc. Far East
P.O. Box 13998
Salem, OR 97309-1998
inquiries@crimethinc.com

www.crimethinc.com

*Printed in Canada by unionized printers
on 100% post-consumer recycled paper.*

As usual, we looted the crypts of Percy Shelley, Oscar Wilde, Fredy Perlman, and other unfortunates too dead to defend themselves (*see Plagiarism*), as well as some who still draw breath: Alphonso Lingis, Eduardo Galeano, Ursula K. le Guin, Bob Black, Loesje. Let no one say we do not give credit where it is due. Above all, we would like to thank those whose names have not been recorded, predominantly women and poor people and people of color, who provide most of the raw material that reaches us through the works of the acclaimed.

We are all the collective authors of our language and our world, in a continuous collaboration that goes largely unheralded. Those who wish there to be great literature, like those who desire to lead fulfilling lives, have a stake in removing all obstacles to this collaboration, including property rights and coercive power. The foundation of communication itself is the *common,* that which can be shared. For the sake of this principle, we offer this book, like all our works, for the free use of all.

The sheep and the wolf are not agreed upon a definition of liberty.

– Abraham Lincoln

That is to say—the lexicographer presides over a field of struggle as decisive as the workplace or the street.

Dictionaries are closed systems: they are prisons for words. Like human beings, words have to escape or else stifle and die—they must continually reenter circulation beyond the jurisdiction of the experts. Like us, words never fit neatly into the structures designed for them—they always exceed their roles, coming into contradiction with each other and with the logic of the system. There is more in any text than an army of grammarians could name, tame, or codify.

As partisans of *free speech* in the profoundest sense, our task is not to demarcate and police new territories within language, but to blur the lines and offer new points of departure, revealing the antithesis within every thesis and the conflict behind the façade of the commonplace. Refine and redefine: our language, our lives, our world.

CrimethInc. Writers' Bloc

Contradictionary

A B C D E F G H I J K L M N O P Q R S T U V W X Y Z

Abstractions – God, History, Nature, the Future: such abstract concepts open upon infinite horizons. They can only be grasped when they are cut down to a manageable size—for example, in a narrative framed by someone who undertakes to *represent* them. As many people are anxious about these matters, such representatives are in high demand, and wield great influence in selecting what to include in their narratives: "The Lord created Man to be the custodian of His creation," "women are innately intuitive," "the history of civilization is the history of the class struggle." So it is that for God we have priests, for History historians, for Nature scientists, for Revolution theorists—though every human being possesses in his or her own experience alone enough raw material to draw valid conclusions about any of these vast, vague subjects.

Accident – A statistical inevitability.

Some nuclear power plants are built on fault lines, but every mine, dam, oil rig, and waste dump is founded upon a tacit acceptance of the worst-case scenario. On a long enough timeline, everything that can go wrong will, however small the likelihood is from one day to the next. The responsible parties may wring their hands about the Fukushima meltdown—and the Gulf of Mexico oil spill and the Exxon Valdez and Hurricane Katrina and Chernobyl, Bhopal, Haiti—but *accident is no accident.*

ALL ABSTRACTIONS
DEMAND REPRESENTATION

Acephalous – Having no head; e.g., a horizontal federation of autonomous collectives, or an anarchist after an uprising

Adaptation – One develops skills according to one's situation. The executive learns to give orders, the underling to avoid carrying them out; the prisoner becomes adept at doing time.

The drive to utilize one's abilities appears to be at least as powerful as the desire for pleasure. One of the reasons people reenlist in the military—or return to other abusive relationships—is to continue making use of their finely honed crisis management skills. Nothing is more terrifying than the unknown, in which one must become something else—than uncertainty, in which one may blame oneself for things going badly because they really might have gone better. Thus our tremendous capacity for adaptation, though it kept us alive in Auschwitz and Biafra, can shackle us to an otherwise insufferable present.

On the other hand, when we have no choice but to adapt, it is certain that we will. If people survived in Auschwitz and Biafra, we could surely adjust to life without managers.

Addict – The word conjures the image of a shuddering junkie wandering the streets; but anyone familiar with the narcotics industry knows that *selling* is as

The instant you get out of prison you have the sense that you are leaving something dear to you. Why? Because you know that you are leaving a part of your life inside, because you spent some of your life there which, even if it was under terrible conditions, is still a part of you. And even if you lived it badly and suffered horribly, which is not always the case, it is always better than the nothing that your life is reduced to the moment it disappears.

– Alfredo Bonanno

My very chains and I grew friends,
So much a long communion tends
To make us what we are: – even I
Regained my freedom with a sigh.

– Lord Byron

habit-forming as using—and that goes for every other racket as well

Adult – That is to say, obscene

Adventurism – The scandalous practice of enjoying yourself in the course of struggle

Advocate – A lawyer. Hence the redundancy, "devil's advocate."

Afterlife – Heaven is wasted on the dead

Agency – The sense that one is able to exert influence on the course of events. Government departments such as the Environmental Protection Agency retain this word in their names in the same way that an apartment complex replacing a forest might be named "Shady Acres."

Until November 1999, few anarchists knew anything about the World Trade Organization or the International Monetary Fund. Shortly after the historic protests at the WTO and IMF summits of 1999 and 2000, any punk or fellow traveler could expound on their wrongdoings in greater detail than the average grad student. Feeling that one has some leverage upon something, even by proxy or association, makes one a great deal more interested in it.

All this gave Francois a new lease on life. He would shake me and say, "What a ball! Just think! What a celebration if after all this there is not a chance! They are just ghosts, the ones who think people fight to win! *They fight because they like it.*"

– And There Was Light, Autobiography of Jacques Lusseyran, Blind Hero of the French Resistance

Activists usually begin by trying to educate the public in order to build up to taking action. Perhaps they've got it backwards.

Ahistorical – For a century and a half, Marxists have accused anarchists of being ahistorical for prioritizing the same ethical questions year after year. Yet, as Nietzsche said of the Stoic admonishment to "live according to nature" (*see Nature*), we can *only* act, value, theorize historically: every attempt to live according to timeless precepts is shaped by specific historical conditions. The alternative is not historicism, but *opportunism*.

Air Conditioning – The more you use it, the hotter it gets (*see Global Warming*)

Alcohol – A means of reducing inhibitions. Unfortunately, some people's inhibitions are their only redeeming qualities.

Alienation – The distance that separates us from the lives we lead.

A person can survive a day without water, a week without sleep, a month without food. But you can survive alienation indefinitely. That makes it worst of all.

Alleged – Like every weapon, doubt is most frequently wielded against those without power (*see Delegitimization*)

Alternatives – The desiderata of those who hope to enact social change without having to fundamentally alter their way of life. Demanding alternatives often indicates a failure to think outside the framework that produced the original problem.

The equipment is sterilized, the patient is anesthetized, and the operation is about to begin when a deranged man comes charging through the doors.

"WAIT!" shouts the intruder. "DON'T OPERATE!"

"What the hell do you mean, 'don't operate,'" sputters the dumbfounded surgeon. "This woman's life is on the line!"

"DON'T OPERATE!" repeats the hysterical man. "WHAT WILL YOU PUT IN PLACE OF THE TUMOR?"

Amusement Park – What zoos are to animals, amusement parks are to fun

Anarchia – A disorder resulting from too much freedom, first identified by physician and professor

Benjamin Rush. A devout Christian, Rush was one of the Founding Fathers of the United States and is still regarded as one of the most important pioneers in the field of psychiatry. In a review of the effects, as he saw them, of the events of the American Revolution upon the participants, he observed:

> The termination of the war by the peace in 1783 did not terminate the American Revolution. The minds of the citizens of the United States were wholly unprepared for their new situation. The excess of the passion for liberty, inflamed by the successful issue of the war, produced, in many people, opinions and conduct which could not be removed by reason nor restrained by government. For a while, they threatened to render abortive the goodness of heaven to the United States, in delivering them from the evils of slavery and war. The extensive influence which these opinions had upon the understandings, passions and morals of many of the citizens of the United States, constituted a species of insanity, which I shall take the liberty of distinguishing by the name of Anarchia.

Anarchist – In theory, an anarchist is a person who believes that all coercive hierarchy should be abolished in order that everyone might practice complete self-determination. In practice, it matters little what a person believes *should* occur, as even the most

rapacious executives entertain idle notions about how nice things ought to be—couched in hymns about "peace on earth and goodwill towards men," for example. Ideally, therefore, an anarchist would be a person whose every action undermined authority, who seized her destiny in her hands in such a way that others gained control of their destinies as well.

It follows that no one is properly an anarchist, but we can all aspire to anarchism.

Anonymity – Those whose names are always known—not only to their friends and neighbors, but also to colleagues, in-laws, landlords, bosses, potential employers, and law enforcement agencies (*see Facebook*)—must save their freedom of speech for the bathroom wall

Antidepressants – Nowadays, it's too much to ask to be happy. But for the right price, you can be anti-depressed!

Apocalypse – From the Greek *apokaluptein*: "uncover, reveal." The apocalypse is the revelation of all that has been suppressed and invisible, a rupture that shows things as they really are, forcing us to confront what we have been doing all along (*see Climate Change*).

Apparatchik – Professional revolutionaries are to revolution what professional wrestlers are to wrestling

proper. To take the analogy further, episodes such as the Spanish Civil War—in which the communist minority sabotaged the revolution in return for funding from Stalin—show that, as in professional wrestling, the outcomes of struggles involving professional revolutionaries are typically fixed in advance.

Applause – A time-honored means of politely silencing a person who has made enough demands upon the attention of the public; a white noise for dispelling an experience and cleansing the mental palate; a ritual offering audience members a sense of closure so they can forget what has been said and get on with their lives. *If you're happy and you know it, clap your hands.*

Arbitrary – Pertaining to or resulting from arbitration

Aristocracy – From the Greek *aristokratia*: *aristos* meaning "best," and *-kratia* "power." Reputedly, the term originally denoted the government of a state by its best citizens, later by the rich and well-born. The notion of goodness has always been inextricable from power, wealth, and rule (see *Gentle*, *Masterfully*).

Armchair Anarchism – Used properly, just about anything can be a weapon

What do you think an artist is?
An imbecile who has only his eyes
if he's a painter, or ears if he's a
musician, or a lyre at every level of
his heart if he's a poet, or even, if
he's a boxer, just his muscles? On
the contrary, he's at the same time
a political being, constantly alive to
heartrending, fiery, or happy events,
to which he responds in every way.
How would it be possible to feel no
interest in other people and by virtue
of an ivory indifference to detach
yourself from the life which they so
copiously bring you? No, painting is
not done to decorate apartments.
*It is an instrument of war for attack
and defense against the enemy.*

– Pablo Picasso

Army Recruiter – A child predator

Arson – The strategy of a retreating army

Art – Less avant, more garde!

Asymmetrical Warfare – In 2006, three detainees hanged themselves at the US prison camp on the shore of Guantánamo Bay. Their suicide notes were not released to the public. All three had participated in hunger strikes and had been force-fed by camp authorities; deadpan as always, the US military announced that their corpses were being treated "with the utmost respect." Despite their lawyers' insistence to the contrary, Camp Commander Harry Harris told the BBC World News that he did not believe the men had killed themselves out of despair: "They are smart, they are creative, they are committed," he emphasized. "They have no regard for life, either ours or their own. I believe this was not an act of desperation, but an act of asymmetrical warfare waged against us."

Atavistic – When their favorite team wins a championship, mild-mannered accountants build fires in the middle of the street and dance around them

Author – In order to describe the world, he puts himself under voluntary house arrest

Autogestion – This Spanish and Italian word has equivalents in many languages, with the exception of English. It is generally translated as self-management, but it can also imply "giving birth to one's own activities," creating oneself anew in the process rather than simply acting on pre-existing inclinations. At the close of the 20th century, *autogestion* was the watchword of the network of squatted social centers spanning southern Europe; it was embodied in underground popular traditions like anarcho-punk and "extra-parliamentary" political activity that focused on direct action rather than political representation.

The closest English cognate is "autogenous," arising from within.

Autonomist Marxist – Perhaps the most telling difference between Marxists and anarchists is that the former tend to associate themselves with the program of a specific thinker—Lenin, Trotsky, Stalin, Mao, Marx himself—while the latter regard thinking as a collective process, taking for granted that a good line of inquiry doesn't need a big-name theorist to validate it.

This focus on intellectual property and leadership is doubtless interconnected with the authoritarian politics of most self-proclaimed Marxists; neverthe-

less, there are some who maintain that Marxism is compatible with autonomy and horizontality. But it is not enough for them simply to champion autonomy, horizontality, and the revolutionary seizure of the means of production; they still feel the need to drop the name of the foremost authority on communism, like Christians citing the Good Book for legitimacy.

Baby Steps – The biggest steps of all

Bad Neighborhood – In class terms, a neighborhood without a gate; in economic terms, an area where people may gather without spending money; from the vantage point of the white suburbs, anywhere you can see people of color smiling

Bailout – In the words of Benito Mussolini, "Fascism should rightly be called Corporatism, as it is the merger of corporate and government power." This neologism did not take off, however—probably because fascism is not the only political system premised on such a merger.

Balaclava – On October 24, 1854, English, French, and Ottoman forces fought Russian troops north of the port of Balaclava in one of the major conflicts of the Crimean war. The British managed to halt the Russian advance,* but when the British commander ordered the cavalry to prevent the Russians from carrying off the guns they had captured, the commander of the Light Brigade misunderstood. Believing him to intend that the Brigade should prevent the Russians from moving their *own* guns, the commander launched a suicidal frontal attack through a valley surrounded by Russian artillery.

The Light Brigade was utterly decimated, and the commander cantered back alone to enjoy a champagne dinner on his yacht in the Balaclava harbor. The Heavy Brigade, which was commanded by his estranged brother-in-law, had been ordered to follow—but halted at the edge of the valley, its commander not seeing any point in squandering his troops as well. The commander of the Light Brigade was hailed as a hero, while his brother-in-law never recovered his reputation.

The balaclava, a form of knitted headgear that obscures one's identity, is said to take its name from this battle. It has since featured in many similarly courageous and ill-conceived attacks involving an outmatched challenger, as Tennyson mused in his poem "Charge of the Light Brigade,"

Charging an army, while all the world wonder'd.

* This initial British success gave rise to the expression "the thin red line," from which is derived the more recent custom of referring to the police as "the thin blue line" separating civilization from chaos—or the ruling class from justice, according to your vantage point.

The valley of death a year later,
still strewn with cannonballs

Modern applications of the balaclava

Bandwidth – In text messages, the range of expression is narrow: you can use caps lock, but you can't scream; you can use emoticons, but you can't touch. In place of the infinity of embodied experience, our technology reduces the world to binary code. Contrary to advertising rhetoric, the electronic era condemns us to an increasingly low-bandwidth existence.

Beat Cops – Please.

Beat Poets – What the hell, beat them too.

Bewilder – The city boy is *bewildered* in the countryside, just as the landlubber is *at sea* in a boat

Birth Control – In 1914, Margaret Sanger coined the expression "birth control" in the pages of her monthly newsletter, *The Woman Rebel*, to which Emma Goldman and other anarchists regularly contributed. After working as a nurse in New York's Lower East Side, she had concluded that the only way to do anything for the health of poor women was to bring about major economic and social change. The dissemination of birth control methods, which at that time were illegal even to describe, was only one aspect of this project.

This Voltairine de Cleyre quotation in the first issue, explaining the role of violence in the labor movement, is representative of the tone throughout

The Woman Rebel:

> If it's a telegraph strike, it means cutting wires and poles, and getting fake scabs to spoil the instruments. If it is a steel rolling mill strike, it means beating up the scabs, breaking the windows, setting the gauges wrong, and ruining the expensive rollers together with tons and tons of material. If it's a miners' strike, it means destroying tracks, bridges, and blowing up mills. If it is a garment workers' strike, it means having an unaccountable fire, getting a volley of stones through an apparently inaccessible window, or possibly a brickbat on the manufacturer's own head. If it's a street-car strike, it means tracks torn up or barricaded with the contents of ash carts and slop carts, with overturned wagons or stolen fences, it means smashed or incinerated cars and turned switches. If it is a system federation strike, it means "dead" engines, wild engines, derailed freights, and stalled trains. If it is a building trades strike, it means dynamited structures. And always, everywhere, all the time, fights between strikebreakers and scabs against strikers and strike-sympathizers, between People and Police.

After seven issues, Sanger was charged with violating obscenity laws for writing about birth control—and for "inciting murder and assassination." She fled the United States to escape prosecution. Upon her return, she founded the American Birth Control League, and continued to serve as its president after

THE WOMAN REBEL

NO GODS NO MASTERS

VOL. I.   JULY, 1914.   NO. 5.

TRAGEDY

Even if dynamite were to serve no other purpose than to call forth the spirit of revolutionary solidarity and loyalty, it would prove its great value. For this expression of solidarity and loyalty and of complete defiance to the morality of the masters, in a time of distress and defeat and death, is the most certain sign of that strength and courage which are the first essentials to victory. On July 4th, three revolutionists, Caron, Berg and Hanson, were killed by the explosion of dynamite—sacrificed because of their willingness to risk life for their convictions. This tragedy created a wonderful spirit of loyalty and solidarity among their comrades. It ought to have awakened the same spirit among all those who advocate the overthrow of the present system —at least among those agitators and leaders who urge direct and revolutionary tactics against the master class.

But instead we have witnessed a far greater tragedy than the death of our comrades. That event in itself bespoke courage, determination, conviction, a spirit of defiance—unfortunately, unusual qualities. The real tragedy has been the cowardice and the poisonous respectability expressed in the apologies of those adepts in that glib and oily art to speak and purpose not—those agitators and leaders who howl about solidarity among the workers, only to whitewash themselves with respectability when an episode occurs which actually offers an opportunity for the expression of such a spirit of solidarity. Instead of this expected defiance of conventional morality and standards, they have given nothing more than involved, shamefaced explanations and apologies actioned which do more to discredit the organizations they represent than any number of bombs or ill-advised acts of violence.

Explanations and apologies, like patriotism, are the cloaks of cowards, not the reactions of strong men.

It is time to learn to accept and exult in every act of revolt against oppression, to encourage and create in ourselves that spirit of rebellion which shall lead us to understand and look at the social situation without flinching or quavering or running to cover when any crisis arises. Not until we do create this spirit will the revolutionists ever be feared or even respected in America.

We are all talking revolution and direct action, solidarity and freedom. If we are not willing to back every word that we utter publicly by determined action, we will never accomplish anything except to render ourselves ridiculous.

Solidarity is a means, not an end. It will unite the working class against its oppressors not at a single catastrophe at some dim and distant future date, but only as we individually incorporate it. We must Live Solidarity, not merely talk it. Even if we disagree regarding the social value of the act of revolt, we must accept it and acclaim it for the spirit and the motive in back of it. Never repudiate or apologize for the comrade who, by an act of revolt has given the best evidence of loyalty to his class, of his SOLIDARITY.

If the so-called revolutionary labor movement must justify its actions at the bar of the very public opinion and morality that have created and sustained laws against labor, it is a wishy-washy, milk-and-watery, weakness movement at best. If it cannot accept as possible and inevitable and valuable among its ranks such men as Berg, Caron and Hanson—if, in short, it is not moving in the direction of REVOLUTION, it is time for us to build up a movement that is.

A DEFENSE OF ASSASSINATION
HERBERT A. THORPE

It is generally agreed that lower forms of life must give place to higher types, and when the pioneer of civilization makes his way into the forest, he must of necessity destroy the man-killing animals living therein. Exterminating warfare is also waged against the savage members of the human race wherever they oppose the establishment of conditions necessary for the development of the more highly organized types. Of course, where improvement by instruction and subsequent co-operation is possible, this extreme of annihilation need not be practiced, but unless it can be shown that there is room enough on earth for both savage and civilized, the savage must go.

Having thus indicated the operation of the law of the survival of the fittest, it would seem that we should apply the same treatment accorded to wild animals and savage to those men in civilized countries whose nature still display traits characteristic of the tiger and wolf, and who, owing to the nature of our social fabric, are beyond the reach of correction.

It is immaterial whether such men are conscious or unconscious of their true natures and the effect of their actions on others. If their position in modern life is an entirely false one, as in the case of the czar or king, this is their misfortune, but, like the savage member of society, they should not be permitted to live upon or block the march of the many toward better conditions.

There is no difference, ethically, between killing a man instantly or slowly over-working or starving him to death, yet those are the conditions imposed upon millions of workers throughout the world to-day, owing to the brute force of the employing and official classes, and their ability to control large armies of ignorant police and soldiers to intimidate the workers whenever a clash occurs between Capital and Labor.

Another weapon used by these undeveloped czars of industry, whose egoism runs riot, is to dictate to their legislative hirelings what laws shall be enacted, or, if any exist that balk their selfish desires, to coerce their judicial puppets so to interpret them as to nullify the beneficial effect sometimes intended.

The point I wish to bring out is this —that since the great mass of people are by force of circumstances unable to use the same weapons employed by the better educated and privileged class, this does not preclude the working class from using whatever other means of defense may be at its disposal, such as the strikes, boycott, sabotage or assassination.

The assassination of tyrants has been practiced throughout history in all parts of the world, and in regard to nihilism in Russia, Wendell Phillips has this to say: "Nihilism is the righteous and honorable resistance of a people crushed unmore conservative participants managed to rename the organization Planned Parenthood.

Today, despite anti-abortion terrorists murdering doctors and bombing clinics, we take condoms and birth control pills for granted. It's easy to forget that scarcely a century ago, only wild-eyed revolutionists spoke of such things. Had their revolutionary aspirations come true as well, the state could no longer threaten our reproductive rights.

Black Flag – Until they make a darker one, it'll have to do

Black Hole of Calcutta – The British East India Tea Company, one of the most famous international drug trafficking cartels of all time and the de facto corporate ruler of India for over a century, insisted on fortifying a military base in Calcutta over the objections of the locals. In 1756, the Nawab of Bengal laid siege to the fort; the garrison's commander slipped away, leaving former surgeon John Holwell in charge, and the base soon fell. According to Holwell, 146 captives were then imprisoned overnight in the fortress's twenty-foot-square dungeon, subsequently known as the Black Hole of Calcutta, and all but 23 of them were dead by morning.

The story goes that a Bengali landlord, convinced that Holwell had been exaggerating, attempted to crowd 146 of his tenants into an equally tight space and found that he could not. He took this as proof of his hypothesis, pointing out that a Bengali villager's body occupies much less space than a British soldier's—if only because the latter were fattening themselves from the larders of the former. The tenants' feelings about this experiment are lost to history; no doubt the landlord would have been pleased to pack his tenants as tight as his countrymen had once packed the British, if he could have.

There are still black holes in Kolkata and elsewhere around the world, into which disappear the millions who live and die in abject poverty; but their deaths, unlike those of British colonists, go unheralded.

Bling – An expression for expensive, ostentatious jewelry or clothing that entered circulation via hip hop, expanding to cover status symbols of all kinds and the flaunting thereof. As Audre Lorde might have said, the master's jewels will never dismantle the master's house. Hip hop is hardly the only milieu in which status symbols are glorified, unfortunately, although the symbols themselves vary widely from one context to another. For example, anarchists may find this term useful to diagnose their comrades' intellectual pretensions:

"My new 'zine cites, like, Hegel and Butler and Kristeva and Blanchot, too! From the singularity to the totality, I got it all, know't'm saying? Crazy Kabbalistic references and shit!"

"Aw, man, you don't understand any of those motherfuckers! You're just blingin! Seriously, what's any professor ever done to get you up out of your job at the café?"

Blood Bank – Is there any other kind?

Bluff – Near the end of the Second World War, twice-decorated veteran Aleksandr Solzenhitsyn was arrested for sending a letter mentioning "the moustached one," which the censors took to designate Stalin himself. Young Aleksandr was sent to the Soviet prison labor camps along with millions of dissidents, supposed conspirators, prisoners of war, and hapless civilians.

After Solzenhitsyn and his fellow inmates had spent several strenuous months in forced labor, a guard distributed registration cards in a belated effort to sort out who all these new prisoners were. One of the blanks on the form was marked "Trade or Profession." Other inmates answered "tailor," "barber," or "cook" in hopes of obtaining a more advantageous position in the camps; but Solzenhitsyn, fed up altogether, scribbled in "nuclear physicist." At this time, the top Soviet scientists were racing to discover the secret of the atomic bomb.

Solzenhitsyn didn't give the survey another thought, but a year and a half later a Black Maria arrived just for him. It took him to a *sharashka*, a special scientific research facility run by Ministry of State Security. He had never studied nuclear physics.

We can imagine Solzenhitsyn on the laboratory bench the following morning, beginning his first day of work under the watchful eyes of elite guards. Concealing his dismay, he whispers to the inmate beside him, "Are *you* a nuclear physicist?"

"Shh—*of course not,*" hisses back his new colleague. "But don't worry—these morons have no idea what's going on."

Bohemian – Taste makes waste

Border – To create a community where people share no real connection or common interest, establish a boundary and accuse outsiders of violating it. This accusation implies that before the violation, the rightfully included lived together in purity, tranquility, and belonging. There was no such thing as America before immigrants, for example, but you'd never know it listening to racists and nationalists. It is common sense that boundaries create transgressors—but one might as easily say that the invention of transgressors creates boundaries, which would be unthinkable without them.

Bottom-line – The problem with collective projects is you have to do them yourself

Bowdlerize – As soon as Michelangelo was dead, his little-known colleague Daniele Ricciarelli was hired to paint over the genitals in his fresco of the Last Judgment in the Sistine Chapel. Following in Ricciarelli's footsteps, prison reformer Thomas Bowdler is best remembered for *The Family Shakespeare*, a ten-volume collection of the Bard's plays in which "those words and expressions are omitted which cannot with propriety be read aloud in a family." All this happened hundreds of years ago, but today there is still no shortage of philistines who bowdlerize whatever they can get their hands on. You can even find supposed anarchists who think revolutionary struggle would be more appealing without Molotov cocktails, lust for revenge, and unlimited sexual freedom.

Broken Window Theory – The superstition that if minor infractions are aggressively repressed, more serious crime will decrease. Nowadays, this is associated with Rudy Giuliani's brutal tenure as mayor of New York City, during which the New York Police Department grew to be one of the largest standing armies in the world so as to crack down on graffiti and subway fare evasion; but the theory originally appeared in an article by James Wilson and George Kelling:

Consider a building with a few broken windows. If the windows are not repaired, the tendency is for vandals to break a few more windows. Eventually, they may even break into the building, and if it's unoccupied, perhaps become squatters or light fires inside.

Or consider a sidewalk. Some litter accumulates. Soon, more litter accumulates. Eventually, people even start leaving bags of trash from take-out restaurants there or breaking into cars.

There you have it—it's not poverty or homelessness that causes people to become squatters, arsonists, or larcenists, but unrepaired windows. Similarly, Western thinkers as prestigious as Aristotle once believed in spontaneous generation—that aphids arise from the dew that falls on plants, fleas from putrid matter, mice from dirty hay, and so on.

In an interesting twist, ever since the protests at the 1999 World Trade Organization summit in Seattle, anarchists appear to be operating on the same premise: if only a few windows can be broken, revolutionary struggle is bound to break out.

Brotherhood – An imagined ideal relation between all mankind [sic]; the tie that bound Abel and Cain

Bugaboo – An imaginary threat trotted out to keep the timorous in order (*see Fox News*)

Bureaucracy – Rule from behind desks; the infrastructure underpinning every form of government that ends in -*cracy*

Business End – The wrong side to be on, obviously

Capability – One does not suffer nearly so much from one's inadequacies as from one's unused abilities. Consider the frustrated three-year-old, who feels himself to be capable of a great deal more than anyone will permit him to undertake; or the insomniac, who in another era would have protected the clan by standing night watch; or the sensitive soul who cannot make a separate peace with the injustices of this society but is compelled to confront them even when everyone else turns away. Until we find a use for it, our limitless potential is a curse, not a blessing.

Capitalism – Just as monarchy means rule by monarchs and communism means rule by communists, capitalism means rule by capital itself. The wealthy rotate in and out of power, but the accumulation of wealth remains the determining force.

Captive Audience – Once upon a time, this distinction was useful, as other audiences might properly disengage themselves if they so chose; in the age of Facebook and Twitter, the qualifier has become practically redundant

Cardiologist – He knows how to maintain it, but not what it's for

Cargo Cult – The story goes that in the Melanesian Islands of the Pacific Ocean, locals who had experienced limited contact with colonizers engaged in rituals modeled on their behavior in hopes of thus obtaining their technology. Anthropologists and reporters describe islanders building mock landing strips to entice planes laden with cargo, or elevating real or mythological Western figures to the status of Messiah.

It's hard to know how seriously to take this version of the story, in view of the general ethnocentrism of the narrators. In 1964, when the residents of an island off Papua New Guinea rebelled against their Australian rulers by refusing to pay taxes and voting ironically for US President Lyndon Johnson in the island's first elections, this was reported by gullible US journalists as a "Johnson cult."

Perhaps the concept of the cargo cult better describes modern-day developers who expect a thriving economy to erupt anywhere they put a high-speed train, or televangelists who promise material wealth to those who donate to their ministries. Our interpretations of foreign customs always tell us about what is most familiar to us.

Carsick – Sickened by the motion of a vehicle in which one is riding; on a larger scale, sickened by the motion of the vehicles in which others ride (*see Pollution, Greenhouse Effect*)

Caution – Better safe and sorry

Celebrities – If you weren't nobody, they wouldn't be anybody

Censorship – You are not allowed to read what should be written on these walls

Chaos – The sum of all orders

Charity – The means by which those who own everything else attempt to corner the market on benevolence.

It's possible to charge that individual charitable acts assuage guilty consciences instead of solving problems, or distract attention from the roots of those problems—but charity itself, even at its most apparently effective and well-intentioned, is essentially a demonstration of power in a system based on competition and humiliation. In every act of charity, the subtext is that those offering the handouts are so industrious that they can not only provide for themselves—the ultimate measure of worth in this

individualistic society—but also share a surplus with the incompetent.

This is why such assistance is not always received with the anticipated gratitude: in contrast to other kinds of gift-giving, charity glorifies the one who offers it and humiliates the recipient. At bottom, the benefactor is not there to assist the one in need; the one in need is there to confirm the status of the benefactor. The philanthropist gives, but on his terms, emphasizing his property rights and position of privilege. Charity is the opposite of sharing.

Everyone knows that, as a rule, the less people have, the more they're willing to share; this says a lot about the effects of wealth on human beings. In place of charity, we would do well to develop ways of assisting one another in which we share not only resources but also, more importantly, control over them.

Childhood – The heirs of the previous generation's unfulfilled longings prove that they are ready for adulthood by keeping this inheritance intact, so as to pass it along to the next generation with interest

Christmas – An ancient pagan holiday occurring around the winter solstice, celebrating a variety of deities including sun gods, sons of God, and, most recently, Mammon

I fear it is true that there are no children in America.

– Lewis Carroll

Civil Disobedience – Disobey if you must, but for goodness' sake behave yourself

Civil Liberties – The less civil, the more liberties

Civil Society – That is to say, only those who remain civil qualify as society

Civil War – In the United States, people don't revolt in order to obtain freedom, but to continue denying it to others

Civilization – A crime against nature; despite Gandhi's quip, a bad idea;* the tendency of pedestrians to stop walking when they step onto an escalator

* Asked what he thought about Western civilization, the Mahatma famously responded, "It would be a good idea."

Class – Class is not a static identity, but a relationship; it obscures the issue to say a person is of one class or another without reference to immediate economic relations. A person can shift from one position in the class system to another; so can a whole profession. Class interests aren't fixed, either—counting on one class to lead the struggle against hierarchy is bound to disappoint (*see Revolutionary Subject*).

Ninety years after his betrayal and murder at the end of the Mexican Revolution, Emiliano Zapata returns to life somewhere north of the Rio Grande. Immediately, he sets out to raise another army and resume the struggle for agrarian reform. He accosts the first mestizo he sees, an affable grad student at the nearby university: "Discúlpeme, señor. ¿Dónde se encuentran los campesinos del pueblo?"

"Campesinos? I'm not sure we have any campesinos, exactly. Actually, come to think of it, you're in luck this afternoon! It's just a couple blocks away—here, I'll show you."

"Muchas gracias," answers the revolutionary general, taking in the general import of the offer and touching the brim of his sombrero. The two stroll along the sidewalk, passing cell phone shops and haute cafés, to an open area where a vinyl banner proclaims FARMER'S MARKET.

Zapata surveys the scene. "No estoy seguro, amigo," he whispers, fingering his trademark handlebar mustache, "Este mercado está lleno de puros gringos." The student just shrugs, so Zapata strides around the closest table, past a hand-lettered sign reading "Heirloom Tomatoes—$5.99/pound," and addresses the proprietor.

"¡Compañero! ¿Estás cansado de vivir de rodillas? ¿Estás listo para luchar por tu tierra y tu libertad? ¡Juntémonos!"

"No, no, *not here!*" hisses the mortified farmer. "I told you, I'll pick you up at the gas station on Monday morning!"

Clout – A heavy blow with a blunt object; hence, influence in politics or business

Coffin – A parcel marked "Return to Sender"

Coke – A solid fuel made by heating coal in the absence of air; an illegal stimulant derived from coca leaves; a corporate beverage including coca ingredients.* Comparably addictive and deleterious in all three instances.

* Provided by Stepan Company, the only corporation authorized to import coca into the US.

Collaborate – To be, as Milan Kundera put it, "the brilliant ally of your own gravediggers"

Colonialism – In Oscar Wilde's *The Picture of Dorian Gray*, the innocent young protagonist, presented with a lovely portrait of himself, wishes that the painting would age, rather than he. His wish is granted, and as he descends into debauchery, the visage in the painting grows more and more dreadful, while he continues to appear unblemished, above reproach.

Today, comparing Brussels to Kinshasa, one might discern a similar phenomenon, though Belgian rule of Congo ended way back in—1960.

Common Sense – What is common becomes sense, but what is sensible doesn't always become common

Community – The sum of all the individuals and relationships in a social milieu—that is to say, none of them in particular; therefore, the abstraction for which any of them may be sacrificed

Compassion – On March 1, 1881,* after centuries of failed revolutionary movements, after countless dissidents had passed through the gates of the prison of Peter and Paul Fortress never to return, four young

---

* According to the Old Style calendar.

"The good person, if he could see the future, would help to bring about his own sickness and death and mutilation, since he knows that these things are assigned to him according to the order of the universe, and that the whole is superior to the part and the state to the citizen."

– Epictetus, *The Discourses*

I have just returned from a journey inland to the village of Insongo Mboyo. The abject misery and utter abandon is positively indescribable. I was so moved, Your Excellency, by the people's stories that I took the liberty of promising them that in future you will only kill them for crimes they commit.

– Missionary John Harris of Baringa, writing to King Leopold's chief agent in the Congo about the business venture that cost the lives of approximately 10 million people

men took up parcels of explosives and fanned out along Yekaterininsky Canal in St. Petersburg to await the Tsar. They were Mikhailov, a boiler maker; Rysakov, a young student; Grinevitzky, a former engineering student; and Yemelyanov, a cabinetmaker—all members of *Narodnaya Volya,* the People's Will. Many of their comrades had already gone to the gallows; their leader had just been arrested and awaited the same fate.

Mikhailov lost his nerve and dropped his parcel off on his way home. Rysakov intercepted the Tsar's carriage as it turned onto the quay and cast his parcel under the horses' hooves. The explosion knocked him back against the fence and killed one of the guards, but only damaged the bulletproof carriage. But when the Tsar got out to investigate, Grinevitzky leapt forward and detonated his bomb, fatally wounding his target and himself.

Yemelyanov came running up, only to find that there was nothing he could do. Rysakov had been captured, Grinevitzky was done for, and the dying Tsar was crouched in a spreading pool of his own blood, his regal uniform hanging off him in rags. Yemelyanov had sworn through clenched teeth to give his life in return for this man's death, to avenge at any price the suffering inflicted across centuries of monarchy. But seeing his mortal enemy reduced to his knees, weakly calling for help, the desire for revenge evaporated. Tucking the volatile package under his

arm, he hurried to the Tsar's side and tearfully lifted him into a sleigh so he could be borne back to the Winter Palace to die.

Were it not for the bombs, Yemelyanov would never have been able to approach the Tsar, let alone assist him. Where there is such hierarchy, what extreme measures are necessary for human beings to be able to show compassion to one another!

Complicity – Domination is a relationship, not a condition; it depends on the participation of both parties. Hierarchical power is not just the gun in the policeman's hand; it is just as much the obedience of the ones who act as if it is always pointed at them. It is not just the government and the executives and the armed forces: it extends through society from top to bottom, an interlocking web of control and compliance. Sometimes all it takes to be complicit in the oppression of millions is to die of natural causes.

Concessions – As the Empire is overrun by barbarians, the Emperor's scribes franticly record his pronouncements: "I grant Gaul to the Franks! And Iberia to the Vandals! And all the treasures of Rome—as a sign of my munificence—I bequeath to Alaric and the Visigoths!"

"All the treasures of Rome are burning, sire," observes the youngest scribe, marking the Visigoths' progress through the palace window.

"Well then! I'm not the sort of churl who tells my subjects what they should do with my gifts. Take down that I grant the right to burn them, too!"

The authorities don't grant concessions out of the kindness of their hearts; they simply concede the reality of what their subjects are strong enough to compel from them. If you want political leverage, don't beg for it, don't seek it through their channels—take power outside them.

Conflict Resolution – When radicals hold a meeting, they sit in a circle, facing one another; unfortunately, they do the same thing when they form a firing squad.

One would expect anarchists, being proponents of cooperation and mutual aid, to excel in conflict resolution. Sadly, the opposite is often true: being specialists in opposition, they put more energy into opposing each other than into undermining the systems that rule them.

Conformity – In Rabelais's *Fourth Book of the Heroic Deeds and Sayings of the Noble Pantagruel*, our heroes are circumnavigating the globe when they encounter a French merchant vessel. One of its passengers, a sheep seller traveling with his flock, insults Pantagruel's friend Panurge, taking him for a fool. Counseled not to make a scene, Panurge responds by respect-

fully inquiring as to whether he can purchase one of the merchant's sheep, picking out a particularly fine specimen.

The merchant continues to mock Panurge as they haggle over the price, but Panurge pursues his object, repeatedly bringing the conversation back around to business. The merchant explains how his flock is descended from the ram that provided the Golden Fleece sought by Jason and the Argonauts; how their dung cures seventy-eight different diseases, and their horns make asparagus sprout from the ground; he calls Panurge a cuckold, a dolt, a prize idiot. Panurge patiently insists that he wishes to make a purchase.

Finally, the merchant accepts Panurge's money and hands over his object—the biggest, fattest ram in the flock. Panurge immediately lifts it into his arms, carries it to the edge of the boat, swings it back, and hefts it over the railing into the ocean.

All the other sheep, seeing their leader disappear from view, charge forward and begin to hurl themselves two and three at a time into the frothing sea. The merchant watches, his face ashen, as his fortune disappears into Davy Jones' locker. Finally regaining his wits, he rushes into the fray to stop them, and is borne overboard in a blur of bleating and wool. Panurge watches dispassionately. It doesn't pay to depend on the impressionable.

Confusion – In June 1937, asked for his feelings about the Spanish Civil War, Alduous Huxley wrote,

> My sympathies are, of course, with the Government side, especially the Anarchists; for Anarchism seems to me more likely to lead to desirable social change than highly centralized, dictatorial Communism.

He can be forgiven the non sequitur, for people who called themselves anarchists had indeed joined the Republican government. The mystery is not how he was confused, but why they were.

Consensus – If only everyone always agreed, there would be no danger of oppression—but that's a totalitarian fantasy, not a formula for liberation

Conspiracy Theory – Like free enterprise, conspiracy can be good, theory can be good, but conspiracy theory is not so good

Contempt of Court – A healthy sentiment (*see Hung Jury*)

Contranym – A word that is its own opposite (*see Child Care, Commonwealth, Justice of the Peace*)

Control – Order reigns but it doesn't govern

Convert – As a verb, it is used by basketball coaches discussing how to make the most of a gambit, as insurgents might also aspire to do; as a noun, it describes something unspeakably obscene

Conviction – A firmly held belief, or the quality of demonstrating that one is firmly convinced of what one believes; hence, the legal repercussions thereof

Co-op – A cooperative venture; alternately, a typographical error for "co-opt"

Corner the Market – Generally, it's the other way around

Coronation – A ritual formally asserting a monarch's God-given right to be shot, stabbed, poisoned, guillotined, or blown up with dynamite

Couple – A safe, non-reactive romantic configuration. Chlorine is a poison gas and sodium an explosive metal, but together they make table salt.

In monogamous circles, singles are seen as unpredictable elements: lacking something, they may take dangerous steps to get it. Even the government appears to regard singles as a potential liability—hence, presumably, the tax incentive for getting married. Couples, on the other hand, can be trusted to keep each other in check.

Cowardice – The defining character trait of those who singlehandedly take on the assembled forces of their society, as diagnosed by fearless prosecutors and judges

Criminal Justice – Some judges are so corrupt, no amount of money could sway them from delivering unjust verdicts

Critique – At first, one only recognizes particular instances to be worthy of critique; critique appears synonymous with rejection, implying deficiency in the object. Over time, one discovers that *everything* warrants critique. This can produce cynicism: nothing is above reproach, nothing is pure, therefore nothing has value. But followed through to its logical conclusion, this insight inspires a profound optimism: if everything can be critiqued, then no matter how bleak things are, there is always a way to improve them.

Those who comprehend this can pass beyond the binary of approval and disapproval to identify the conflicting currents within any subject of inquiry. There are sides to take *inside* every position, as well as between them.

Cultural – Of or pertaining to cults, large or small

Customer – In our country, only one custom persists

If you want to make a difference, have the courage to say how the life you lived was the life of a coward.

– Judge Ann Aiken, sentencing Daniel McGowan to seven years in prison with a terrorism enhancement*

---

* After a career of environmental activism and direct action, Mc-Gowan had been arrested by the FBI on arson charges. Though prosecutors threatened him with a sentence of life plus 335 years, he refused to inform on his codefendants even as most of them turned state's evidence in the course of a year-and-a-half-long legal ordeal.

One can't help wondering what Judge Aiken would be capable of on the other side of the bench. Would she still insist on due process of law, urging others to be patient as people were sold into slavery or carted off to Dachau? *Cowardice* is an interesting choice of words for a professional whose complicity in the status quo is rewarded with physical safety, financial stability, and social status. Would Aiken have lectured John Brown about cowardice, or the Germans who attempted to assassinate Hitler?

We live in a democracy, Aiken might counter: bypassing the established channels and breaking the law is akin to attacking freedom, community, dialogue itself. That's the same thing they said in 1859.

Dandy – Nowadays, they're called hipsters

Data – In a world reduced to 1s and 0s, everything is fungible (*see* Statistics, Rivers of Blood)

Deadline – Historically, the *deadline* was the line around a prison beyond which prisoners were eligible for shooting. In keeping with shifts in the exercise of control, what once was delineated spatially over life is now enforced temporally over labor.

Death Penalty – The fact that the state occasionally takes life wholesale can't help but discourage people from complaining about the economy taking their lives piecemeal. The former practice is regarded as barbaric, of course, so it is generally inflicted upon those who have been demonized as more barbaric: "Sure, it's scary that we have so much power that we can kill you if we want—but wouldn't it be worse for monsters such as this one to have that power over you?" The average politician owes a lot to rapists and murderers—without them, he might have to answer for the subtler atrocities he countenances.

Debate – An opportunity for mutual gain often mistaken for a competition, to everyone's misfortune; as in economics, those who set out to win doom all to losing. Nothing is more precious to someone

"So long as I don't have to see it!"

who wishes to sharpen her analysis and expand her perspective than an intelligent person who disagrees with her.

A rhetorician can dominate an argument; a bore can win the field by attrition; an ideologue can stop up his ears and perhaps also the brains of everyone in earshot. But if you wish to converse rather than compete, you have to shoulder the burden of helping your interlocutor make her argument, as well.

Deceit – In 1968, inspired by Sir Francis Chichester's solo voyage around the world, nine extraordinary characters set out to circumnavigate the earth alone in the *Sunday Times* Golden Globe Race. This was the first competition of its kind. Today's open-ocean races are dominated by yachts owned by Rolex and BMW, with handsomely paid crews and the best engineering money can buy; the Golden Globe competitors were eccentric amateurs piloting small vessels.

On the last possible day for departure, weekend sailor Donald Crowhurst limped out of the small town of Teignmouth in a tangle of sails, lines, and wires. Crowhurst had outfitted his vessel with a variety of his own inventions, including a balloon intended to turn the boat upright should it capsize; he hoped the voyage would render these marketable, though many of them never worked at all. His boat, a custom-constructed three-hulled sailboat named the

Teignmouth Electron, had not been properly prepared for open sea travel, and Crowhurst himself had never sailed such a vessel before. He fell off the boat three times before embarking.

Crowhurst had staked everything on this race. If he didn't complete it, he would have no way to pay off the debts he had brought upon his family. Yet within the first few weeks, as his inventions failed and the *Electron* began falling apart, it became clear that even finishing last was beyond his abilities.

The South Atlantic, towards which Crowhurst was sailing, is a vast and terrifying expanse. Unhampered by land, the seas there are whipped by monstrous storms; the latitudes are described without exaggeration as the roaring forties, the furious fifties, and the screaming sixties. With his boat rapidly taking on water, Crowhurst knew that attempting to brave the passage would be suicide.

But with his family's finances in the balance, failure was not an option. Crowhurst began to make false logbook entries charting an imaginary voyage, conveying this story to the papers back home in short, vague radio transmissions noting how smartly his boat was sailing. He attributed his long radio silences to faulty equipment and reported speeds that broke world records. To his supporters, it appeared that Crowhurst's luck had changed. As the world imagined the *Teignmouth Electron* battling the gales around the Cape of Good Hope, the tempests of the Indian Ocean, and the doldrums of the open sea, Crowhurst bobbed around the Atlantic logging his invented itinerary and fleeing whenever he spotted another vessel.

His plan was to finish last in hopes of avoiding scrutiny, but one by one all the other competitors dropped out until Crowhurst was one of only two left in the race, his false reports forecasting him frontrunner for best time. Worse, the *Electron* was in no condition even to sail back to Teignmouth without repairs that would require a stop ashore, strictly forbidden by the rules of the competition. Crowhurst nervously put in on the Argentine coast, managing to conceal his presence from local officials, and set out to return to the harbor from which he had started.

All England waited to welcome home a hero, with fleets of boats to usher the knight-to-be into port. Crowhurst could anticipate intense press coverage; his contracts required him to write about the voyage and to produce footage from the trip. He would also have to present his carefully falsified logbook to the officials for review, some of whom were already dubious.

Out in the Atlantic, Crowhurst began frantically scribbling in a third logbook. He called this one his philosophy; its contents bear all the signs of madness. In page after page of disordered ramblings about the human condition, Crowhurst attempted to theorize his way out of the hole he had dug himself into, only to return to the hopelessness of his situation. "There can only be one perfect beauty," he wrote in anguish: "the great beauty of truth."

On July 1, 1969, after over half a year in isolation with his own duplicity, Crowhurst made his final log entry; his abandoned boat was found nine days later, adrift in the Atlantic. It is presumed that he finally resolved his difficulties by stepping off the sailboat into the all-absolving sea. The last entry in his logbook reads, "IT IS FINISHED—IT IS FINISHED. IT IS THE MERCY."

Somewhere in the eighth circle of inferno, where Dante put deceivers and falsifiers, Donald Crowhurst still sails in circles, a real-life Flying Dutchman doomed never to return to port, patron saint of those whose efforts to evade their day of reckoning only compound their troubles. May we all own up to our fibs and fabrications before we join him in hell's deep.

Decimate – Literally, to kill one out of every ten, as the Romans would do to punish a mutinous legion. Presumably the risks of obedience had been computed to be slightly less.

Defendants – Remember, even the innocent ones may have done nothing wrong

Degenerate – The accusation of *degeneracy* has a richer history than most would care to remember.

In the mid-19th century, Italian doctor Cesare Lombroso was the first to use this expression as a medical term for physical and moral deterioration. In studies of anarchists such as Sante Caserio, the assassin of French President Sadi Carnot, Lombroso argued that some people are born criminals whose crime-prone natures correlate with abnormal physical characteristics by which they can be detected and preemptively weeded out. Theft was not a desperate response to hunger, nor anarchism a social movement—rather, both were symptoms of an incurable medical condition.

Max Nordau developed Lombroso's pseudoscientific ideas into a critique of modern art. In his 1892 book *Entartung*, he argued that contemporary artists were suffering from mental pathology and disorders of the visual cortext. Though Jewish—Nordau helped found modern-day Zionism—he decried their work as inferior to traditional German culture, a theme that National Socialists appropriated wholesale a generation later.

The Nazis used the term *degenerate* as a blanket condemnation of any movement that manifested symptoms of "cultural decline," including Expressionism, Dada, Surrealism, Cubism, Atonality, Serialism, Jazz, and Primitivism, as well as anything made or owned by Jews, radicals, and "sexual deviants." In 1937, the

The artist does not work for the artist, but like everyone else he works for the people! And we shall take good care that from now on the people will be the judges of his art.

– Adolph Hitler, quoted in the *Entartete Kunst* exhibition guide

German government began purging such artwork from museums and seizing it from individuals. Over 16,000 works that had been considered modern masterpieces were removed from museums. About 650 paintings and sculptures were selected from among these for a massive exhibition entitled *Entartete Kunst*—"Degenerate Art"—to be mounted in Munich.

The exhibition was designed to ridicule "degenerate" works, promoting the idea that modernism was a conspiracy by people who hated German decency. The artists were frequently identified as "Jewish-Bolshevist," though only six of the 112 artists represented in the exhibition were Jewish. It was held in cramped, badly-lit rooms separated by temporary partitions; paintings were crowded onto the walls and identified by handwritten signs. Descriptors such as "Insult to German Womanhood" and "Mockery of God" were scrawled on the walls, and actors were hired to behave like madmen and incite the onlookers with insulting remarks. Minors were banned from the exhibition on the grounds that it would corrupt them.

Despite all this, *Entartete Kunst* was arguably the most widely viewed modern art exhibition of all time. Over two million people attended it in Munich and it toured Germany and Austria for three years after its premiere, during which another million saw it. An exhibit of "Great German Art"—art exemplifying the "Heroic" realist style favored by the Nazis—that opened the day before only attracted 420,000 viewers, though it was located just around the corner.

After the exhibition, much of the artwork was destroyed. The Berlin Fire Department burned 5000 paintings in 1939; others were auctioned to foreign buyers, the profits going to the Nazi regime. The artists whose work had been included in the exhibition were blacklisted as enemies of the state; they were forbidden to make artwork and subjected to surprise Gestapo raids to ensure that they complied. Many escaped into exile. Countless others were imprisoned or killed in concentration camps in Germany and Eastern Europe. One bitter joke of the time declared that "half the Berlin Symphony is in Auschwitz."

In every charge that art is incomprehensible and elitist, there is an echo, however faint, of Nazi rhetoric about degeneracy. Foes of hierarchy rightly reject the valorization of art that is opaque to the uninitiated over the creative activity of common people—but the implication that all art should be accessible to all is borderline fascism, even when it is framed as class-conscious populism. A variant of this charge is the shock self-professed philistines express upon learning the price of a canvas they regard as a glorified cleaning rag.* In fact, the Nazis set the precedent for this complaint,

* An anti-capitalist might counter that all prices of all commodities, from the cheapest can of beans to the most expensive Van Gogh, are equally absurd.

too: paintings in the *Entartete Kunst* exhibition were labeled with the prices for which they had previously sold, although many of these prices had been set in the period of post-war inflation when the Deutschmark was worth a fraction of its value in 1937.

Why did so many people attend the Munich exhibition? *Entartete Kunst* was simultaneously the most popular and most despised art exhibition ever staged. Is it more fulfilling to be outraged than to be moved? Do gallery-goers and theater patrons today also crave reassurance that they are superior to the eccentrics who entertain them? Perhaps many who attended the exhibition came instead to say goodbye to the artwork they loved and the era that was passing with it. Whatever their motives, they failed to save the art or the artists who created it—an important lesson about the solidarity between creators and audiences.

And why did the Nazis focus so much attention on art and music? It's telling that they went to such lengths to suppress experimental composers as well as avowed political dissidents: this indicates that they saw convention-defying expression itself as a grave threat to their program of domination. Indeed, art, music, and poetry were used by those in ghettos, in concentration camps, in hiding, and in exile as weapons for survival and revenge. As the exhibition guide put it, *Entartete Kunst* was intended "to expose the common roots of political and cultural anarchy"—roots

Entartete Kunst

vom 11. November bis 31. Dezember
im Ausstellungshaus der Schul-
verwaltung, Spitalergasse

that anarchists should not overlook today.

Finally, why did the attempt to do away with "degenerate art" fail? Most of the art movements the Nazis opposed are more acclaimed today than they ever were in their era, while the Third Reich—widely approved in the 1930s—is remembered as the nadir of human history. Is this only because the Nazis were bested in the contest of arms that followed their repression of defenseless artists and musicians? Or does art itself possess offensive capabilities beyond simply ruffling the feathers of the bourgeoisie?

Delayed Gratification – Tomorrow will use you the way you use today

Delegitimization – "Self-proclaimed," "self-described," likewise "rambling." Of course, anyone with the attention span fostered by today's media would find *War and Peace* rambling.

Delusion – As sadism is named for the Marquis de Sade and masochism for Leopold von Sacher-Masoch, reading Deleuze produces a certain condition

Democracy – As Oscar Wilde put it, "The bludgeoning of the people by the people for the people." A system that promises everyone the opportunity to rule everyone else, yet renders no one free.

Our forebears overthrew kings and dictators, but they didn't abolish the institutions by which kings and dictators ruled: they *democratized* them. Yet whoever operates these institutions—be it a king, a president, or an electorate—the experience on the receiving end is roughly the same. Laws, bureaucracy, and police came before democracy; in democracy as in dictatorship, they function to interrupt self-determination. The only difference is that, because we can cast ballots about how they should be applied, we're supposed to regard them as *ours* even when they're used against us.

Three wolves and six goats are discussing what to have for dinner. One courageous goat makes an impassioned case: "We should put it to a vote!" The other goats fear for his life, but surprisingly, the wolves acquiesce.

But when everyone is preparing to vote, the wolves take three of the goats aside. "Vote with us to make the other three goats dinner," they threaten. "Otherwise, vote or no vote, we'll eat *you*."

The other three goats are shocked by the outcome of the election: a majority, including their comrades, has voted for them to be killed and eaten. They protest in outrage and terror, but the goat who first suggested the vote rebukes them: "Just be thankful this is a democracy! At least we got to have a say!"

SHUT UP
AND VOTE

Denial – In this day and age, a certain kind of illiteracy is a prerequisite for business as usual (*see The Writing on the Wall*)

Dependence – After simmering years of censorship and repression, the masses finally throng the streets. The chants echoing off the walls build to a roar from all directions, stoking the courage of the crowds as they march on the center of the capitol. Activists inside each column maintain contact with each other via text messages; communications centers receive reports and broadcast them around the city; affinity groups plot the movements of the police via digital mapping. A rebel army of bloggers uploads video footage for all the world to see as the two hosts close for battle.

Suddenly, at the moment of truth, the lines go dead. The insurgents look up from the blank screens of their cell phones to see the sun reflecting off the shields of the advancing riot police, who are still guided by closed circuits of fully networked technology. The rebels will have to navigate by dead reckoning against a hyper-informed adversary.

All this already happened, years ago, when President Mubarak shut down the communications grid during the Egyptian uprising of 2011. A generation hence, when the same scene recurs, we can imagine the middle-class protesters—the cybourgeoisie—will simply slump forward, blind and deaf and wracked by seizures as the microchips in their cerebra run haywire, and it will be up to the homeless and destitute to guide them to safety.

Desire – In evolutionary terms, human beings do not have desires in order that we might fulfill them and be happy, but to propel us over obstacles. This is evident in the way desire increases in proportion to the difficulty of its object—a misfortune for most, but a tremendous boon to romantic poets.

Despair – Those who give up hope don't usually cease to respond to the forces that act upon them; on the contrary, defying those forces requires extravagant reserves of hope (*see Hunger Strike, Desertion, Refusal*). Rather, they continue to respond to them, while ceasing to invest their actions with meaning. For most of us, resigned to living without any great stakes, nihilism would be something to aspire to. In the suburbs, hell is overhead.

Determinism – The French astronomer Pierre-Simon Laplace speculated that if we could know the precise location and momentum of every particle in the universe, we would be able to deduce the entirety of the past and future. Scientists and philosophers have bickered about this ever since.

Certainty, there's something reassuring about the

idea that the future is already written, inevitable and inexorable, even if it is a worst-case scenario. Without this certainty, facing the horizon of an unpredictable future, we have to confront the twin possibilities that everything depends on us, and that everything we do is utterly insignificant—to act as if everything depends on our decisions, without *needing* that to be the case.

Development – The forest before us, the desert behind

Dictatorship of the Proletariat – (*see* *Dictatorship*)

Difference Engine – A primitive draft of a modern mechanism for producing uniformity

Digitization – Centuries hence, some unfortunate families will pass down the hereditary role of guarding nuclear waste burial sites to protect the unwary; others will become the custodians of the last libraries of the old world. Visiting pilgrims will wander those dusty stacks, marveling at Icelandic sagas and National Geographic coffee-table books, noting how printing quality dropped toward the end of the industrial era, and wondering about the terrible cataclysm implied by the historical record breaking off at 2014.

Disappear – Not so long ago or far away, outspoken opponents of the ruling order simply vanished. This was eventually deemed heavy-handed; today, more care is taken to ensure that they do not appear in the first place.

Of course, when radicals don't even attempt to make their case to the general public, secret arrests and executions are unnecessary: for all practical purposes, they are already *disappeared*.

Discovery – The process by which all that was previously known is forcibly erased (*see New World*)

Discussion – An answer perpetuates a question; a deed supersedes it

Dishwashing – Some necessities transcend specific social systems. Until the last dish is washed in the blood of the last manager, you can be sure the dishwasher's hands are clean.

Disillusionment – We still build Towers of Babel; we've just given up on reaching heaven

Disincentive – "Abolish the commodity society!" exhorts the would-be revolutionist. "Abolish the society, commodity!" the economy mocks back. "Or try—and if you fail, headstrong little product, we'll cut your market value 50%!"

The Dishwasher's Guide to Politics

Capitalism: You wash the dishes, the ones who own them profit

Libertarianism: You wash the dishes, the ones who own them profit tax-free

Democracy: Even as a dishwasher, you deserve a say as to which politician is best suited to protect the economy that keeps you in the kitchen

Nationalism: Forget about those dishes for a second—you're a citizen of the proudest nation on earth!

Fascism: The Mexicans who washed the dishes are deported, the Jews who owned the place are imprisoned, and everyone else is conscripted for military service

Unemployment: The only thing worse than being trapped in the dish room is being trapped outside it

Neoliberalism: The dishes are shipped overseas to be washed and you're free to develop your own combination of Unemployment and Nationalism

Reform: Shorter stacks, warmer water, longer breaks—same dishes!

Socialism: Dishwashers' wages increase just enough to afford higher taxes

Communism: From each according to his means, to each according to his need—as determined outside the dishroom

Marxism: Between shifts, the dishwasher studies the intricacies of dialectical materialism. It turns out that thanks to his efforts, the dirty dishes have been accumulating value for his boss to invest in more dishes. The stuff about the dictatorship of the proletariat is more confusing, but the party theorists reassure him that it makes perfect sense to them. Under their direction, he joins his fellow dishwashers in a risky coup d'état. Afterwards, he is distraught to find himself still in the kitchen, washing dishes for party bureaucrats. The bureaucrats reassure him that they will eventually wither away.

Syndicalism: The dishwashers join labor syndicates that send representatives to a council, at which it is decided which dishes are to be washed and when

Anarcha-Feminism: You wash dishes for the boss— who washes the dishes at home?

Anarcho-Primitivism: Down with dishes!

Anarcho-Punk: Down with washing!

Insurrectionary Anarchism: A quixotic attempt to distill a political theory from the practice of smashing dishes

Anarchism: Everyone shares in the dishwashing

Disorder – A disruption of the anarchy that otherwise characterizes our world. Any organically ordered system—a rainforest, for example, or a circle of friends—is an anarchic harmony that tends to perpetuate itself through constant change; disorder, on the other hand, can only be maintained by ever-escalating exertions of force. The precarious discipline of a high-school classroom, the factory farm in which sterile rows of genetically modified corn are defended against weeds and insects by a host of technological innovations, the fragile hegemony of a superpower—these are not examples of order, but of disorder imposed from above.

Some confuse disorder with anarchy, misunderstanding it as the absence of any system. But disorder is the opposite of anarchy: enforced over a long enough period of time, it systematizes itself, stacking up hierarchies according to its pitiless demands. One of the most advanced forms of disorder is capitalism: the war of each against all, rule or be ruled, sell or be sold. You could say capitalism is a social disorder in the same way that bulimia is an eating disorder and sickle cell anemia a blood disorder.

Distraction – In summer of 1797, the poet Samuel Taylor Coleridge experienced a vision in which the entirety of the poem "Kubla Khan," consisting of some two or three hundred lines, appeared to him fully formed. Upon waking, he immediately sought pen and paper and managed to jot down fifty-four lines of it before he was interrupted. As Coleridge himself later related,

> At this moment he was unfortunately called out by a person on business from Porlock, and detained by him above an hour, and on his return to his room, found, to his no small surprise and mortification, that though he still retained some vague and dim recollection of the general purport of the vision, yet, with the exception of some eight or ten scattered lines and images, all the rest had passed away like the images on the surface of a stream into which a stone has been cast, but, alas! without the after restoration of the latter!

And so the poem, which even in its unfinished state is arguably among the best compositions in the English language, was lost forever.

Nowadays, the people from Porlock don't have to come by in person to detain you about their Business. They can call you on the phone, send you an email, text message you, instant message you, page you, tweet at you, address you over an intercom or loudspeaker, bark at you out of one of the television sets that hang in airports and gas stations, waylay you via a billboard or radio commercial, even send you a singing telegram. Small wonder if poetry is in decline—Porlock has us surrounded.

Disturbing the Peace – Interrupting the war

Divorce – You never truly know someone until the two of you have been through a messy breakup

Do – Just as one tends to project the attributes of one's acquaintances onto abstract characterizations of "the" people, it is common to generalize one's own activity as universal. "Do it yourself" means repair your own gutters or publish your own 'zine, depending on whom you ask. When the singer of a Swedish metal band screams "Do it!" he's announcing a guitar harmony in minor thirds, while arch-Yippie Jerry Rubin once used the same phrase to call for the opposite of what Nike meant by their derivative advertising slogan,

Not how one soul comes close to another but how it moves away shows me their kinship and how much they belong together.

– Friedrich Nietzsche

"Just Do It." "We did Quebec City last April and we're doing Cancún next fall" implies something entirely different coming from a bourgeois tourist than from a summit-hopping anti-globalization activist. When a frat boy says "I'd do her," he indicates that he can only see members of the so-called opposite sex as placeholders in a sexual competition with his brothers. When Lenin asks *What Is to Be Done?* you know the answer is bound to be bad news.

Likewise, whom one is speaking to—or which aspects of their character—fundamentally determines the meaning and consequences of an exhortation. INDULGE YOUR DESIRES comes across very differently on a billboard advertising SUVs than it does spray-painted across the broken windows of an SUV dealer. It follows—note well, theorists!—that what you say is not nearly as important as how and where you say it.

Domestic Violence – One almost doesn't dare leave the streets

Domesticated – Civilized; that is to say, neutered, declawed, and dependent

Domestication – Everything they do to humans, they test on animals first

Doom – Forget about storing up treasures for the future, whether in retirement or revolution (*see Delayed Gratification*); the earth is going to be eaten by the sun. The last act of every play is already written.

Double Bind – If we didn't steal from our bosses, we couldn't afford to pay our landlords

Downgrade – Arago's claim that Pope Callixtus III had Halley's comet excommunicated appears to be apocryphal, but in August 2006, the International Astronomical Union formally demoted Pluto from planet proper to dwarf planet. Even celestial bodies have less job security in the Information Age than they did under religious rule.

Downtown – No one goes there anymore—it's too crowded

Drapetomania – A mental illness causing African slaves to attempt escape, described in 1851 by physician Samuel Cartwright in his report "Diseases and Peculiarities of the Negro Race." Not surprisingly, Cartwright prescribed whipping as the most beneficial treatment. One can't help wondering what perspective the passing of time may give on the disorders diagnosed in our own era.

**ALL
SHOWS
CLOSE**

Dream – A crime against reality

Driver's License – What they drive with in Rome
(*see Artistic License*)

Duty – The Nuremberg defense

Eco-terrorism – A word coined by the Center for Defense of Free Enterprise. Just as those whose lands were stolen via violent conquest and violated treaties are "Indian givers," those who would prevent the destruction of those lands are "eco-terrorists."

Economics – Communism didn't work, capitalism doesn't work—*you* work. When will it end?

Economy – As an adjective, "cheap"; as a noun, that which compels us to render ourselves thus

Editor – A sort of King Midas who shoulders the thankless task of turning literary lead into gold; a paragon of humility no less than genius, qualified to be the supreme arbiter of taste, economy, and style; an august personage who blesses ungrateful hacks with priceless insight and expertise—whatever the original author of this definition might say

Educate – (*see Reeducate*)

"What a pity—not enough *education*."

Education – Just as some liberals seem to think everyone could be a professor if only people would stay in school long enough, some radicals seem to think all that is lacking for revolution is for the masses to be sufficiently educated in radical theory. On the contrary, it is practice that teaches.

Eleutherophobia – The fear of freedom—a phenomenon better known by other names

Enantiodromia – The tendency of things to change into their opposites, especially as a supposed governing principle of natural cycles and psychological development. Prefigured in Heraclitus, this idea reaches us by way of Carl Jung, in his *Aspects of the Masculine*:

> Enantiodromia. Literally, "running counter to," referring to the emergence of the unconscious opposite in the course of time. This characteristic phenomenon practically always occurs when an extreme, one-sided tendency dominates conscious life; in time an equally powerful counterposition is built up, which first inhibits the conscious performance and subsequently breaks through the conscious control.

Perhaps this explains the Neoconservatives, who began as liberal socialists and ended up masterminding the War on Terror, or the German "Anti-Deutsch," who began by opposing Germany's legacy of anti-Semitism

Victory will not go to those who can inflict the most suffering, but to those who can survive the most

and ended up supporting the War on Terror as it targeted Arabs in an updated form of anti-Semitism. Certain insurrectionists may also be expressing this principle in their transition from rejecting all coercive force to affirming antisocial violence of all stripes.

Every position that does not encompass the whole is forced to coexist with its opposite. Those who cannot acknowledge this *become* their own opposites.

Endurance – The anvil seems to be getting the worst of it, but the hammer breaks first

Enemies – If you are a warrior, the nature and scale of your enemies will determine the nature and scale of your actions. In this sense, it is even more important to choose your enemies wisely than your friends.

Entelechy – The realization of potential, a word as unfamiliar to modern readers as the practice it describes

Enterprise – People who get up early in the morning cause poverty, pollution, and genocide

Entitlement – While the privileged generally feel entitled to do as they please regardless of the consequences for others, the oppressed often find it more difficult to justify asserting their interests. Consequently, they sometimes contrive elaborate legitimizations of their desires in the terms of their oppressors.

Following the death of Tsar Ivan the Terrible in 1584, rule of Russia passed into the hands of the aristocrat Boris Godunov. All Ivan's children were dead by the end of the century; Dmitri, the youngest, died of a stab wound under suspicious circumstances in 1591.* However, twelve years later, a young man appeared in the west who claimed to be Dmitri, declaring that he had escaped assassination and was returning to claim his rightful throne. Godunov's regime was widely hated, and supporters flocked to the standard of the new Dmitri; townspeople across southern Russia overthrew their local governments and pledged allegiance to him, pinning all their hopes on his insurgency. After Godunov died in 1605, a great part of the armed forces changed sides; finally, the population of Moscow rose up and toppled the government, welcoming Dmitri as the new Tsar. The mother of the original Dmitri accepted him as her son, and many others vouched for his authenticity.

Less than a year later, Dmitri was assassinated in an aristocratic coup, and his body exhibited in Red

---

* This marked the end of the dynasty founded by the legendary Rurik in the 9th century, though centuries later the anarchist Peter Kropotkin could trace his lineage to that chieftain. Kropotkin's fellow revolutionists teased that he had more right to the throne than Tsar Alexander II of the ruling Romanov family.

Square. Yet announcements and letters continued to appear in the murdered Tsar's name, and the southern provinces returned to rebellion. An escaped slave named Bolotnikov, carrying a letter in Dmitri's handwriting proclaiming him commander-in-chief, took charge of the rebel forces; soon half the nation was in their hands, and they laid siege to Moscow. Dmitri himself did not appear, but captured rebels swore to the death that he was alive.

At length, the siege was broken, and Bolotnikov's forces were themselves besieged. In fall 1607, when they were on the verge of defeat, a man professing to be Dmitri appeared in the west, convening another army. Bolotnikov arranged to turn himself over to the authorities in return for his soldiers going free; he was imprisoned and murdered, but his men flocked to the new Dmitri, and soon Moscow was once again besieged.

The siege lasted for a year and a half. In 1608, Dmitri's wife arrived at the rebel camp and recognized the new Dmitri as her murdered husband. Even after this Dmitri was killed in December 1610, it was only a few months before another appeared. The unrest continued until Poland and Sweden invaded and the Russian ruling classes were finally able to consolidate control in the course of mobilizing a nationalist defense.

Many historians regard the string of Dmitris as nothing more than the repetition of a cynical ploy, but one could also interpret Tsar Dmitri as a collec-

I wish to be free.

Only the Tsar is free.

Therefore, *I must be the Tsar!*

tive identity, a myth any rebel could incarnate. For example, after Dmitri was assassinated in 1606, his friend Molchanov "became" Dmitri just long enough to inspire a new outbreak of resistance. Later that year, "Tsarevich Petr," a poor cobbler's son who assumed power among the rebels by identifying himself as a fictitious relative of the slain leader, nonetheless set out in search of him—even though Dmitri had been killed twice by then, and doubtless would have known that he had no nephew Petr! Likewise, when Petr was killed, a "Tsarevich Fedor" appeared at the head of 3000 Cossacks, claiming to be Petr's younger brother; it also turned out that the nonexistent Tsarevich had an uncle, "Tsarevich Ivan-Avgust." Dozens of other beggars, peasants, and escaped slaves became real or invented noblemen via this kind of transubstantiation, and—more strikingly—were accepted by their countrymen as such.

Perhaps, in such a stratified society, it was easier for an entire nation to convert to a sort of magical realism than for the oppressed to rise up in their own name. As peasants and slaves, their agency was meaningless, illegitimate; but as the Tsar, or at least warriors in his service, they became literally entitled to it. Despite their tribulations under the autocratic system, it came more naturally to found a struggle upon the impossible fantasy of a just, rightful Tsar than to reject Tsardom altogether.

All this begs the question—what Tsar is *not* an imposter?* How does blood lineage, or divine right, or for that matter the electoral process, qualify a person to rule others? It may be that, as faith in the validity of the Tsar's power was itself supernatural, common Russians were open to further supernatural developments relating to the Tsar—especially if those happened to validate their own rebellious desires. On the other hand, some historians speculate that the first person to appear as the resurrected Dmitri was so persuasive because he had been raised from childhood to believe he was the rightful inheritor of the throne. What would it take to raise an entire people to feel similarly entitled to their agency, royal blood or no?

The idea of the rebel Tsar as a manifestation of divine authority among the common people, butchered by earthly authorities yet miraculously surviving,

---

* In a surreal bid to undercut the cult of personality around the dead leader, the aristocrat who seized power after Tsar Dmitri's assassination presented the corpse of a dead child as the disinterred, miraculously preserved body of the original boy Dmitri, and ascribed additional miracles to the Tsarevich. He forced the Orthodox Church to grant sainthood to the Dmitri who had died in 1591, and made Dmitri's mother, who had so recently accepted Tsar Dmitri as her son, announce that this was her true son's body. Government forces were blessed in the name of "St. Dmitri" before going into battle; thus, in fall 1606, the rebels and the government faced off under the standards of two false, dead Dmitris.

echoes the story of Christ. Indeed, this period of Russian history brings to mind the Anabaptist uprisings in Western Europe of the preceding century, in which peasants justified armed struggle in apocalyptic religious terms. Both upheavals attest to the power of myth to enable people to pass beyond self-imposed limits, but also reveal how mythologies framed in the rulers' terms impose limits of their own. Until the oppressed feel entitled to act for themselves without reference to divine ordainment, hereditary rights, legal statutes, humanitarian responsibilities, or grand historical narratives, they will only be able to borrow the paltry freedom of their oppressors.

Entrap – When federal agents, being too incompetent to catch anyone actually involved in criminal activity, need something to show for all their efforts, they seduce unwary victims into compromising situations and arrest them (*see Eric McDavid*). Technically, this is illegal—but like anarchists, federal agents don't trouble themselves about trifles when there's a job to do.

Épater les Bourgeoisie – The timeless pastime of filthy, promiscuous, drug-addicted perverts

Equality – A glass ceiling we can all bang our heads on in unison

Il faut épater le bourgeois.

– attributed to Charles Baudelaire

Escalate – An escalator is a machine that carries a person closer to Kingdom Come; practiced thought-lessly, escalation adds up to the same thing

Evangelist – "Once, I was a lost soul. I had pro-miscuous sex, I was addicted to drugs, I stole and blasphemed and disrespected my parents. But then I accepted Jesus Christ as my Lord and Savior, and dedicated my life to spreading His Word!" He moved on to the really hard stuff.

Evolution – Why your parents never understand

Exclusion – Shut doors = broken windows

Exercise – From time to time, a postman would appear from among the trees to the West, staggering under a great load. The foreigner still received mountains of correspondence: he was bombarded with commercial offers, leaflets, catalogs, luxurious temptations from the consumer civilization from which he had defected.

On one occasion, he found in the mass of papers a special offer for a rowing machine. He showed it to his neighbors, the fishermen.

"Indoors? They use it indoors?" The fishermen couldn't believe it. "Without water? They row without water?" Their amazement increased. "And without fish? Without sun? Without sky?"

The fishermen emphasized that—while they got up every morning before dawn and put out to sea to cast their nets as the sun rose over the horizon, and this was their life and this life pleased them—rowing was the one infernal aspect of the whole business: "Rowing is the one thing we hate," they all agreed. The foreigner explained that the rowing machine was for exercise.

"For what?" asked one robust, sun-bronzed fisherman.

"For exercise," repeated the foreigner, and took a breath, preparing to describe how his countrymen rode elevators and escalators and moving sidewalks and subways and cars to the gym to work out on treadmills and stationary bicycles, to explain gym memberships and personal trainers and the careers necessary to pay for them—but thought better of it. "You know—customs, rituals, ceremonial rites."

"Barbarians!" The fishermen shook their heads.

Exogamy – The custom of marrying outside a clan or community. This ancient tradition has something to offer today's aspiring revolutionaries: closed circuits are for electronics, not social movements.

Experience – Note on a locked door: "Applicants for wisdom—inquire within"

Expiation – Who is going to heaven is a religious question—likewise who is in the right, who is most radical, and how much suffering the guilty deserve. The more pressing question is how to change things here on earth.

Exploitation – After seizing control of the factory, the workers march to the owner's neighborhood, accompanied by their husbands, wives, friends, and children. They tear down the fences of his gated community and pour through its quaint streets, a riotous torrent clamoring for vengeance. The security guards withdraw in fear as the mob approaches; by the time it reaches his house, the owner is long gone.

On the return journey, one former employee sets down his new wide-screen television to slap a mosquito on his arm. His son, lugging an armful of groceries, is surprised: "Wow, dad, that mosquito had a lot of blood in him."

"That's not his blood, son," his father responds. "That's *my* blood."

Expropriation – If property is theft, expropriation is a settling of accounts. It's said that capitalists will sell you the very rope with which to hang them, but only—the adage fails to note—at a price you cannot afford. That's where expropriation comes in.

Liberals, who accept the capitalist line that a social group only deserves to wield as much power as it has access to funds, show this by focusing their fundraising efforts on their own kind. Anarchists, on the other hand, may gather resources wherever there is a great concentration of them serving no good purpose.

Extortion – The common denominator of all transactions under free market capitalism and state communism

Extreme – Only those prepared to go too far will learn how far they can go

Extremism – A few years into the 21st century, the Dutch corporate media ran a series of stories accusing the squatting movement of escalating violence and criminality. This was bewildering: twenty-five years earlier, squatters had regularly engaged in pitched battles with police, but by the time of the news coverage the movement was comparatively tame and weak. In 2010, following up on the public relations work carried out by corporate journalists, the Dutch parliament made squatting illegal.

When the squatting movement had been at its peak and thousands of people routinely participated in violent confrontations with the authorities, it was impossible to brand it "extremist" because so many people were involved that it was understood as a part of Dutch society. Ironically, it was the decline of such tactics and organizing that enabled the press to brand squatters extremists, paving the way for their formal criminalization. Faced with this smear campaign, the only hope for the squatting movement would have been a resurgence of widespread participation in confrontational activity. This should serve as a warning to all who react to corporate slander by distancing themselves from militant organizing.

Faction – One might speculate that there is an inverse relationship between the momentum of a movement and the number of distinct factions within it. In times of upheaval, everyone focuses on events, arguing about tactics and strategy; in such periods, sweeping tides often wash people from one camp into another, blurring boundaries and shifting stances. On the other hand, when there is little going on, all the exciting verbs of resistance stabilize into nouns; then, radicals differentiate themselves by adopting static ideological positions. These positions serve as a sort of compensation: unable to engage in the activities they desire, frustrated revolutionists satisfy themselves by constructing speculative taxonomies of utopia (*see Hypertrophy*). Yet this tends to put off the general public, who know that the vast possibilities of life cannot be encapsulated in mere isms.

Such factionalism was famously satirized in the March 1913 issue of *The Masses*:

> "A Syndicalist, you know, is a Possibilist Anarchist, just as a Socialist is a Possibilist Utopist, but a Syndicalist is an Antistatist, whereas a Socialist is a Statist and a Political Actionist, only an Antimilitarist and Pacifist. I'm a Collectivist Revisionist myself. Now, it's a funny thing, but my brother claims to be a Hervéist, and says he's a Possibilist Sabotist, but at the same time an Extremist Communist and a Political Actionist … I don't think that's a possible thing, do you?"
>
> "I thought he was a Chiropodist," I said.

Indeed, whatever he may have fancied himself, we fear the fellow in question was simply a chiropodist with a big vocabulary.

Fair – Short for fair-to-middling—in other words, mediocre (see *Fair Trade*, *Fair Use*)

Family – Once, a mutual aid society established by nature herself; today, a miniature state ensuring that each generation grows up accustomed to hierarchy and abuse, or, at best, a sort of reservation to which any compassionate impulses can be quarantined. Should a well-meaning parent not wish to be deputized to perpetuate this state of affairs, the children can always be held hostage (see *Child Protective Services*).

Newborn
Your enemies hold you
Through my arms

Equality

Love

Fellowship

Self-
Determination

Faith

Freedom

Security

Truth

Culture

Family Values – All I learned to do at home was lie, all I learned to do at school was cheat, all I learned to do at work was steal

Fantasy – The one bona fide opposition to reality

Fashion – It's different every season, but it's always the same

Feminism – Well-adjusted women seldom make history

Fiction – Theory, which is supposedly universally applicable to reality, drains itself of the particular to achieve this (*see Abstractions*); fiction, to succeed, must evoke an unreal particular in such a way that it resonates universally. Theory offers truths that lie; fiction offers lies that tell the truth.

Filth – In the words of anthropologist Mary Douglas, dirt is "matter out of place": that is to say, filth is a moral category rather than a physical condition. Small wonder it is associated with immigrants, poor people, manual laborers, hoboes, dissidents, and the insane. One might as easily consider deodorant, perfume, aftershave, hair gel, and other chemical additives *out of place*, along with concrete and asphalt.

Billions of showers and no one's clean

Foolishness – Your average dumb idea attracts only dumb adherents, but some ideas are so dumb that you have to be extremely intelligent to talk yourself into them (*see Categorical Imperative, Historical Materialism, Transhumanism*)

Forgiveness – Once you are no longer immediately threatened by your enemies, it is unbecoming to hate them, let alone slaughter them after the fashion of Joseph Stalin. On the contrary, one of the best reasons to stand up for yourself is to free yourself from the desire for revenge.

Sentenced to death in three countries, the infamous revolutionist Mikhail Bakunin finally managed a

Making itself intelligible is suicide for philosophy.

– Martin Heidegger

daring escape from captivity in Siberia. As soon as he was safely in Japan, he sent a letter to General Korsakov, the Siberian governor, acknowledging that his getaway was bound to be a setback to the governor's career and emphasizing that he did not intend it as a personal slight. He apologetically explained that there was going to be a revolution, and it would be irresponsible for him to sit it out in Siberia where he could not be of use.

Founder – As a noun, the originator of an organization or effort; as a verb, what ensues when this person departs

Free Trade – A source of slave labor; a means of turning rainforests into junk mail; an oxymoron

Free Will – Those who live under capitalist democracy accept its premises of their own free will. Of course, "your money or your life" is a choice, too.

Freedom of Speech – A device for conditioning people to speaking without acting (see *Free Speech Zone*)

Freegan – In the 1940s, needing a term to designate complete abstention from animal products, Donald Watson gutted "vegetarian" to coin the word "vegan." In the 1990s, anticapitalists suspicious of the expanding market for "cruelty-free" commodities adjusted this neologism to "freegan" to describe the total avoidance of exchange economics. But in a world still dominated by capitalism, many other marketplaces loom beyond the marketplace proper—the marketplace of ideas, for example, in which some self-professed freegans decided they should sell the idea of not buying things.

A decade later, freeganism had been covered in dozens of newspapers, radio shows, fashion magazines, and television programs. Of course, in order to fit the story into the narrative of the corporate media, it was necessary to emphasize that freegans were neither homeless nor destitute: freeganism was a political statement, a canny improvement on bargain-hunting, or simply another lifestyle preference, but in any case nothing that would discomfit bourgeois viewers. No desperate expressions of need here! As it turns out,

"If you want to immobilize a person, ask him to speak more on a subject. The more he speaks, the less immediate his need to act will be."

even garbage is granted legitimacy and value sooner than the *people* thrown away by the capitalist system.

We can imagine an officer of the NYPD, having watched one of these instructive news programs, accosting a homeless person rummaging in a trash can: "Hey—get outta there, you! Don't you know there are nice college students who depend on that for food?"

Friendly Fire – War is so cuddly these days (*see Smart Bomb*)

Gallows Humor – Revolutionary, facing the guillotine: "We die because the people are asleep. You will die because they will awaken!" Executioner: "Don't put all your heads in one basket!"

Garbage – Everything subtracted from the present is added to the future with interest

Garnish – Deduct money directly from a person's income to settle a debt or claim. They garnish our wages; we garnish their profits.

Gated Community – To remain stable, oppressive structures must confine the natural inclination human beings feel towards sympathy and generosity to carefully delineated spaces (*see Family*)

We have guided missiles and misguided men.

– Martin Luther King, Jr.

Gentle – As in *genteel* and *gentleman*; the gentleman may do much gently that would be read as mayhem and murder were the poor responsible. Violence is not an objective category of activity, but a set of class prescriptions coded into our very language.

Getaway – Getting caught is the only punishable offence

Ghetto – One can highlight the essential difference between fascism and capitalist democracy by contrasting the ways ghettos are established under the two systems. Under fascism, people are forced into ghettos by the state; under capitalism, people populate ghettos of their own free will by choosing to be poor.

Gift Shop – Yet another contradiction in terms

Global Village – Not long ago, professional football fans who visited certain parts of Africa would notice a surprising number of people wearing shirts advertising teams that had lost the Super Bowl. This was because every year, in preparation for the big game, corporations would print tremendous quantities of shirts for both teams; at the conclusion of the game, the winning team's shirts immediately went on the market while the other shirts were shipped overseas to the losers, globally speaking, presumably as a tax write-off. When the capitalist village is globalized, the wrong side of the tracks encompasses entire continents.

Global Warming – Who knew a few gas stations could turn the world into a gas chamber?

Gluttony – In a scarcity-based economy, the only thing more stressful than having nothing is having something, for one must rush to devour or secure it before others can wrest it away; always consuming and hoarding, one develops nasty habits, and eventually cannot share even when it is necessary for survival

Gossip – A thousand years ago, the word was *godsibb*—in the same sense that one could have a godmother, one had god-siblings; hence, six hundred years ago,

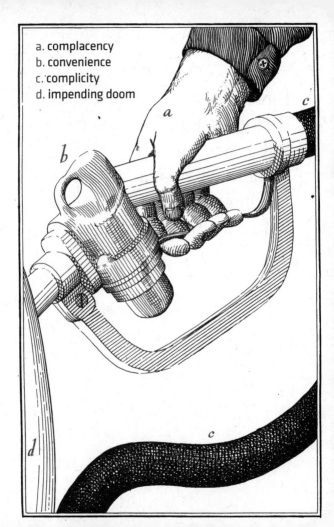

a. complacency
b. convenience
c. complicity
d. impending doom

There is a period when it is clear
That you have gone wrong
But you continue.
Sometimes there is a
Luxurious amount of time
Before anything bad happens.

– Jenny Holzer

a *gossip* was a close friend. Communication carried on by friends outside the formal power structure posed enough of a threat that in the 19th century the powerful redefined it as idle chatter or unconfirmed speculation. Thus men deride women's gossip, which can undermine patriarchal authority; employers prohibit gossip, in which people are judged according to criteria other than how much revenue they bring in; and monotheistic religions classify gossip as a sin alongside pride and deceit.

Of course, the original function of gossip presupposed consistent and meaningful social ties. In the absence of those (see *World Wide Web*), it produces all sorts of bizarre effects.

Graveyard Shift – Capitalism puts some people six feet under without even killing them

Guardian – That is to say, warden

Guerrilla Gardening – So little terrain is left to the contemporary guerrilla, she can barely engage in the most innocuous activities

Guile – A more determinant factor in conflict than brute force.

A high-ranking samurai once had to cross a broad river in a ferry with a bunch of commoners. Surrounded by such insignificant people, he became magnanimous, and began to entertain the unfortunates around him with tales of his courage and military prowess.

The pauper next to him did not appear particularly impressed, however. After regaling him for several minutes, the exasperated warrior finally burst out, "And you? What do you do?"

"Oh, I'm a samurai too," the little man answered.

"You, a samurai? Ho ho!" scoffed the samurai, splitting his sides laughing. "Who is your master, then?"

"Me? I have no master," replied the old man, unconcernedly.

"He has no master! Ha ha! Well then what kind of samurai are you?"

"I'm a swordless samurai."

This gave the warrior pause, for as a child he had been told stories about the Swordless Samurai, a legendary order reputed to be virtually invincible. "You're hardly a bundle of sticks in a burlap sack!"

"Since you insist on insulting me, I fear I must challenge you to a duel."

"You? You—ho ho—challenge me? Ha ha!"

"Fine then, if you will not fight, you may apologize."

The nobleman was enraged. "Oh, I'll fight! You think I'm afraid of *you*? I could snap you in two with my fingers! Name your terms!"

"I have only one. It would be irresponsible of us

to fight here in this boat—we would endanger the civilians around us. Let us fight in the water, if you are really such a mighty warrior."

By this time, the ferry had reached the middle of the river, where the current was strongest and the black water extended around them in all directions. Undaunted, the warrior stood up, placed his hand upon the hilt of his katana, and leapt from the prow, crying out "Come on then! I'll chop you to pieces!"

But the swordless samurai only waved to him pityingly as the river bore him away.

Guilt Trip – A liberal vacation

Gun Control – A measure to ensure that guns always point one direction

Hack – Program or be programmed

Handout – Individual private property quixotically used to obscure the misfortunes caused by the institution of private property

Haunt – Once upon a time, things were older than us, even synthetic things; they arrived in our lives rich with history, bearing blessings or curses, infused with the spirit of those who came before us and charged with their unsettled accounts. Now, instead of ghosts,

our prefabricated houses are haunted by the absence of history, of all meaning whatsoever.

Heart Attack – Without natural predators, even our internal organs are turning on us

Heartbeat – A disorder afflicting an otherwise healthy corpse

Hedonism – If you don't live it up, you'll never live it down

Heterosexual – Straight and narrow

Hierarchical Power – A consolation for having no say in your own life

Highway Robbery – Once upon a time, independent businessmen would halt vehicles on country roads and demand a fee from the occupants; nowadays this industry has been nationalized

History – There are lies, damn lies, statistics—and history

Hogwash – Police testimony (*see Whitewash*)

Home Demo – In activist argot, a demonstration

at the home of a corporate executive or otherwise offensive personage. In carpenters' trade jargon, the act of demolishing everything in preparation for building anew. May the twain meet.

Homeland Security – They slaughter the original inhabitants, poison the water and soil, impose general amnesia, and call this *their* homeland!

Hooliganism – Football was extremely popular in Egypt under the dictatorship of Hosni Mubarak; Mubarak himself encouraged this as a way to build national spirit and channel attention away from his repressive regime. Because dissenting political organizations were prohibited, intrepid young Egyptians flowed into networks of *Ultras,* fanatical football enthusiasts. During games, these "apolitical" groups engaged in increasingly open conflict with the police. When the revolution broke out in January 2011, they were at the front of the clashes, and their songs and cultural signifiers spread far and wide along with the street-fighting tactics they had developed.

In the ferment of social upheaval, energy sublimated into vicarious pursuits returns to real concerns—while the apparently irrational violence of marginalized groups can become a gift to all, reintegrating excluded sectors of the population and excluded practices, such as self-defense, into public life.

The more they tried to put
pressure on us, the more we
grew in cult status. The Ministry
and the media, they would call
us a gang, call us violent . . .
It wasn't just supporting a team;
we were fighting the system
and the country as a whole. Our
role was to make people dream,
letting them know if a cop hits
you, you can hit them back.

– Egyptian Ultra from Al Ahlawy,
quoted by CNN

Hostis Humani Generis – "The Enemy of Humankind," a legal term designating those who are outside the protection of any state or law and may be killed by anyone at any time. Historically, it has chiefly been applied to pirates, who were considered fair game for any noose on account of having *declared war on the world.* Here, once again, the institutions governing humanity are conflated with humanity itself (*see We*); rebels who oppose them come up against the whole species, starting with all who wish to see themselves as its protectors.

Humanity – The most depreciated commodity

Hung Jury – Small fry. Better the judge and district attorney!

Hunger Strike – A time-honored tradition by which the imprisoned express solidarity with their long-suffering supporters

Hustler – His first and last victim is—himself

Hygiene – An ascetic regimen designed to weaken children's immune systems, discourage them from interacting with the natural environment, and deprive them of the information and pleasure otherwise communicated by pheromones

Will arrive soon;
don't wash.

– dispatch from
Napoleon Bonaparte
to his lover Josephine

Hypertrophy – When an organ or capability atrophies, it degenerates from lack of use: for example, those who rarely speak about their desires may lose the ability to frame questions about what they really want, just as those who avoid conflict may not be able to defend themselves. When an organ or a capability hypertrophies, it grows out of proportion to other organs or capabilities, often at their expense; for example, those who speak more often than they act may find that their entire lives recede into theory, while those who focus on confrontation at the expense of building ties may one day look around in desperate need of comrades only to discover that they are alone.

Hypochondria – "Oh my god—I'm afraid I'm coming down with—**HYPOCHONDRIA!!**"

Hypocrisy – Your average good citizen accepts that laws are necessary to keep people in line, while circumventing the ones that are inconvenient for him. Everyone thinks he is the exception to the rule—but who is ready to take exception to being ruled?

Iatrogenic – A medical term indicating an ailment caused by a cure, such as impotence induced by antidepressants, addiction to prescription painkillers, or dependence on indoor heating and air conditioning. "There was an old lady who swallowed a fly…"

Foremost among today's iatrogenic (doctor-induced) diseases is the pretense of doctors that they provide their clients with superior health. This, while new sicknesses are constantly defined and institutionalized, and the cost of enabling people to survive in unhealthy cities and sickening jobs continues to skyrocket. The monopoly of the medical profession now extends over an increasing range of everyday occurrences in every person's life, and preservation of the sick life of medically dependent people in an unhealthy environment has become its principal business.

– Ivan Illich, *Tools for Conviviality*

Identity – A construct for emphasizing the differences between one designated group and others (*see Border*) while suppressing and obscuring the differences between individuals within those groups (*see We*)

Ideologue – Ideas get the proponents they deserve

Ideology – What remains when all lived experience has been extracted from ideas

Ignorance – In Delhi, the poor must walk everywhere, pushing through the crowds that throng the sidewalks—and dwell on them. Here, one sees poverty close up: festering injuries, untreated illnesses, chronic malnourishment, despair and desperation. Those with a little money in their pockets can ride in a rickshaw or taxi, rendering the streets a less troubling blur. The truly wealthy move in limousines and private airplanes from one walled bubble to another (*see Mediation*), shielded from everything so they can speak unironically of investment opportunities while millions go hungry; as their vehicles belch exhaust into the outside world, they literally breathe different air than the unfortunates around them.

Contrary to bourgeois mythology, the greater a person's wealth and privilege, the less likely it is that he or she will be well informed. Privilege means insulation from the effects of one's own actions as

ANARCH
CAPITAL
COMMUN
FUTUR
POST-MODERN
PRIMITIV
SOCIAL
SURREAL
SYNDICAL

ISM

well as other inconveniences; often, those who contribute the most to suffering and devastation are the least aware of it. Who knows more about waste treatment facilities—the people who discuss them in boardrooms, or the ones who live in their shadow?

Imaginary Friend – Every aspiring revolutionary has a favorite imaginary friend, be it the workers favored by labor organizers, the rustics preferred by environmentalists, or the extras from hip hop videos that insurrectionists picture joining them in the streets. Such comrades are much easier to work with than flesh-and-blood human beings; unfortunately, they don't always come through when it counts.

Immediacy – Stories have the greatest impact on those who tell them, magazines on those who publish them, records on those who record them, pictures on those who paint them. Participatory decision-making, the decentralization of power, and the abolition of the division of labor follow naturally from this basic principle.

Immure – Surround with walls; imprison. Once upon a time, only convicts were said to be immured; today one rarely hears this word, perhaps because there are walls enough for all of us.

LIKE THE BERLIN SOMEDAY
THIS WALL WILL BE ONLY
IN MUSEMS.

How to remove
politicians from office

Impeachment – A symptomatic treatment for a systemic problem

Inclusion – There are two ways to approach social change. One is to abolish the existing systems entirely and start over from scratch. The other is to presume that they are essentially good, that they would serve everyone if only they could be expanded to be more *inclusive.* Do we want a guaranteed income, or the abolition of capitalism? Do we want universal citizenship, or the abolition of the state? Do we want a world in which everyone is middle class, or a world in which *no one* is?

The story goes that a well-meaning non-profit organization once raised enough money to supply all the children on a certain destitute island with laptop computers of their very own, reasoning that the single greatest obstacle facing them was exclusion from the World Wide Web. The laptops arrived and were distributed at the school to much rejoicing. But when the children plugged them in and tried to turn them on, the island's power grid was overloaded and shut down. On a global scale, not only is it questionable whether we *should* all wish to be middle-class consumers, it is doubtful that we *could* all be.

Indian Giver – Talk about adding insult to injury!

Indoctrination – Without verbs, slogans are beyond contradiction: "war on terror," "military intelligence," "information superhighway"

Inevitability – Neither death nor taxes!

Infantilize – He calls you sister, but you have to be his mama and his baby

Infidelity – Some allege that polyamory is simply a way for sexist men to have sex with a lot of women without being accountable to any of them. This is unusual, considering that overt polyamory seems to be most prevalent in contexts in which women are empowered and accountability is valued at a premium. In fact, traditional patriarchal social forms (*see Monogamy*) already offer sexist men a model for having sex with different women without being accountable, which has served them well enough since the days of the Old Testament.

Infiltration – Some of my best friends are cops

Inflation – It isn't that commodities are worth more and more; it's that we're worth less and less

Information Age – Information everywhere, communication nowhere

The value of
information does not
survive the moment in
which it was new.

– Walter Benjamin

Inhibitions – As if prohibitions weren't enough

Innocent Bystander – A contradiction in terms

Inquisition – So long as power is concentrated in the hands of a few, inquiry is never impartial and disinterested, nor without consequences

Insurance – A form of gambling in which you bet on your own losses and squander your entire outlay if nothing goes amiss. Paradoxically, when it comes to choosing an insurer, your best bet is to find one who underestimates the risks you face, while correctly appraising those threatening other customers—lest your provider run out of money before your hoped-for misfortune occurs.

In former times, insurance is reputed to have taken less sophisticated forms, such as neighbors taking up emergency collections. Surely, profit-driven strangers are more reliable.

Integration – Like it or not, capitalism is the most successful project of *integration* in human history (*see Inclusion*): it has incorporated all of us into a single global body, in which individuals have increasing mobility while inequality itself is more and more permanent. Perhaps those who struggled for civil rights would have been better off seeking *autonomy* and the power to defend it.

Intern – During the Second World War, it was deemed expedient to intern Japanese residents of the United States in camps, not unlike the forced labor camps overseas. Today, when the foremost threat to capitalism is a restless surplus population for whom it cannot provide salaries or steady economic positions, the *interned* provide free labor to the economy, on the premise that one day there will be jobs enough for them.

Internet – From the capitalist perspective, the ideal product would derive its value from the unpaid voluntary labor of the entire human race, yet be impossible to access except via a line of additional products; without it, it would be increasingly difficult to obtain employment, stay informed, or maintain social ties; and to top it off, it would be hailed as a breakthrough for communication and equality

Intransigence – I'll compromise myself however I must to avoid making compromises

Invention – Mother of necessity

Invincibility – The NATO bombing of Yugoslavia in 1999 quickly decimated most of that already beleaguered nation's defenses. Serbian soldiers with antiquated weapons helplessly awaited their fate while undetectable airplanes rained bombs upon them.

Sophanes, the Athenian, most distinguished himself in the battle . . . He wore an iron anchor, fastened by a brass chain to the belt that secured his breastplate; and this, when he came near the enemy, he threw out, so that when they made their charge, it would be impossible to dislodge him from his post. As soon as the enemy fled, he would take up his anchor and join the pursuit.

–Herodotus, *The Histories*

Determined to keep his crew safe, lieutenant colonel Dani Zoltán insisted that his anti-aircraft group change location constantly, relying on landlines and foot messengers for communication. When they deployed on the evening of March 27, 1999, to his surprise a stealth bomber appeared squarely in the middle of his radar screen. The radar system was a vintage model from 1970; it seemed like it must be an error, but suspending disbelief, he fired up the obsolete surface-to-air missile launcher and took a potshot at the ghost in the sky. Overhead, the US Air Force pilot was jerked out of a pleasant reverie by the shocking realization that two Soviet-era missiles were headed directly at him. He ejected just in time to avoid going down in flames with his 45-million-dollar aircraft.

Stealth bombers cannot be detected by modern radar systems, but Dani had tuned his anachronistic rig to an unusually low frequency, at which the bomber was visible enough. The following week posters appeared across Yugoslavia reading, "Sorry, we didn't know it was invisible."*

---

* Gentle reader, please don't misunderstand our recounting of this tale as approval of the Yugoslav government or military, or any government or military. Our sympathies lie with those who oppose all bombings, and with the unknown wit who painted "Dear president, you were not at home when we needed you most" on a Belgrade wall shortly after his residence was bombed.

Irony – The most popular anarchist anthem of the Spanish Civil War, "A las Barricadas," takes its melody from an older Polish revolutionary song. Written in the 19th century during Russian rule, "Warszawianka" sustained several generations of rebels in the struggle against bosses and foreign occupiers:[†]

> March, march, Warsaw!
> Let's tear off the crown of the Tsars,
> When the people must wear the crown of thorns.
> Let's drown their rotten thrones in blood,
> Already stained with the people's blood!
> A dreadful revenge for today's tormentors,
> Who suck the life out of millions.
> Vengeance for the Tsars and plutocrats,
> And we'll reap the harvest of the future!

Fast-forward through the strikes and street fighting of 1905-1907, through the bloody World War fought on Polish soil, through the Russian revolution and Polish independence—and then through another invasion, another war, another occupation. After the Second World War, the communists who had hummed this song through years of darkness finally held power—and Poland was a satellite of the Soviet Union in the new Russian empire, the Eastern bloc.

† To convey the precarity of Polish identity, it suffices to recall another song: the Polish national anthem, which begins "Poland has not *yet* been destroyed…"

In this new context—a reprise of the old context—we can be sure that the Soviet Union's celebrated Red Army Choir came to Warsaw to perform. Thousands would have poured out to see them, even if attendance had not been compulsory—only a few dissidents were missing. For the encore, the Choir performed their Russified version of the "Varshavjanka"—a popular standby in Moscow, for which a film about the October Revolution had been named.

Imagine the Poles dutifully singing along, dabbing their eyes lest anyone question their loyalty! Here it was, the triumph of internationalism and the proletariat: communism, long sought by both peoples, had prevailed, bringing them together to sing in brotherhood. But on Russian tongues, this song of the underdog was grandiose, smug; the Russians were gloating, daring the Poles to spend another century in struggle—their own weapons, even their own songs, would always be turned against them. There they stood, row upon row in their best clothes, the revolutionary flag draped across the stage, bellowing at the tops of their lungs the anthem of their perennial defeat. And they sang harder, real tears filling their eyes, vanquished and humiliated, hopelessly calling out for vengeance, as if to rescue the profaned hymn along with their dignity: *We'll show you yet, you bastards, we'll drown your rotten thrones in blood.*

Italics – A sure sign of an author whose writing is *slanted to the right*

Jargon – The first refuge of a scoundrel

Journalism – The world's oldest profession. The madman has lost his wits; the journalist simply sells them.

Jurisprudence – The self-satisfaction of the magistrate who had the good sense to be born on the right side of the defendant's bench

Just Deserts – We'll get what we deserve—thanks in advance

Justice – Police everywhere, justice nowhere

Karōshi (過労死) – Japanese, literally "death from overwork": occupational sudden death. Every year in Japan, hundreds of seemingly healthy *shachiku* (社畜)—"corporate livestock"—die unexpectedly of stress-induced heart attacks and strokes. The high working hours in Japan are comparable to few other "developed" nations, with the exception of the United States, which lacks a technical term for this kind of fatality—since who's living, anyway?

Late Fee – The penalty for refusing to pay in advance (*see Landlord, Interest-Free Loan*)

Laziness – A vice in revolutionaries; a virtue in police officers, security guards, and assistant managers

Leadership – A pathological disorder afflicting social groups, in which the majority cease to show initiative or reflect critically on their actions

Left – That is to say, gauche

Left Wing – According to the historical revisionists of representative democracy, the political spectrum has only one dimension, running from those on the Right who wish for state power to be used to defend the interests of property holders, to those on the Left—who desire the same thing, only for the benefit

If only all Rome
had but one neck!
– Caligula

of the general public.* This terminology dates from the National Assembly that met between 1789 and 1791 in France, with the nobles sitting to the president's right and the commons to the left. Those who remain outside representational politics, by force or by choice, do not figure in this political geography.

Yet there are many other criteria that can be used to chart political differences—see the accompanying diagram, in which political tendencies are plotted on a two-dimensional grid portraying both the degree to which power is shared and the processes by which decisions are made. For additional nuances, one could add a third axis—"good cheer," for example, a quality often overlooked by partisans of all stripes.

Leftism – Causes without effects

Leftist – One ensconced in left field

Legitimacy – When we want to be taken seriously, it's tempting to claim legitimacy any way we can. But if we don't want to reinforce the hierarchies of our society, we should be careful not to validate forms of legitimacy that perpetuate them.

---

* In this framework, if you stray too far in either direction, you arrive at tyranny of some kind; this makes it particularly appealing to those who wish to frame their supposed centrism as the least of all possible evils.

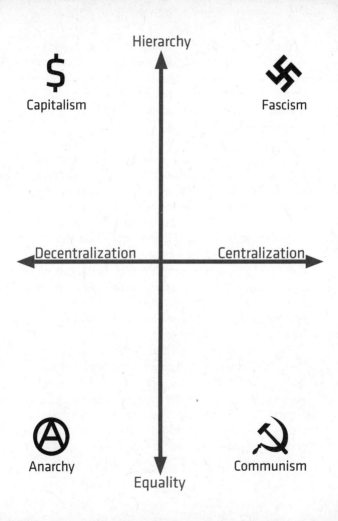

It's easy to recognize how this works in some situations. For example, evaluating people on the basis of their academic credentials prioritizes abstract knowledge over lived experience, centralizing those who can get a fair shot in academia while marginalizing everyone else.

In other cases, this occurs more subtly. Activists emphasize their status as community organizers, implying that those who lack the time or resources for such pursuits are less entitled to speak. Longtime locals claim credibility as such, implicitly delegitimizing all who are not—including immigrants who have been forced to move to their neighborhoods from distant communities wrecked by processes originating in those neighborhoods. People justify their struggles on the basis of their roles within capitalist society—as students, workers, taxpayers, citizens—not realizing how much harder this can make it for the unemployed, homeless, and excluded to justify theirs.

Activists are often surprised by the resulting blowback. Politicians discredit their comrades with the very vocabulary they popularized: "Those aren't activists, they're homeless people pretending to be activists." "We're not targeting communities of color, we're protecting them from criminal activity." Yet the activists prepared the way for this themselves by affirming language that makes legitimacy conditional.

And don't come back until you've done some community organizing!

As soon as the administration learns that one of the buildings has been occupied, the announcement goes out that the occupation is being carried out by *non-students*. At first, this seems like a clever move: in a campus-based struggle, non-student participants are likely to be seen as illegitimate.

In fact, the administration is making a dangerous gamble. By the end of the day, the crowd outside the occupied building has grown to over a thousand people. Does this mean that they didn't hear the announcement, or that they don't believe the administration—or that *they don't care* if the occupiers are non-students? If this sets a precedent legitimizing non-student occupations of campus buildings, it'll be a whole new ball game.

Leninism – If, as Lenin wrote, "Left-Wing Communism" is an infantile disorder, Leninism—the theory of the vanguard party, "democratic" centralism, and the dictatorship of the proletariat—seeks to create an *infantilizing order*

Libertarian – In the United States, a partisan of all the freedom money can buy; everywhere else in the world, a partisan of all the freedom it can't

Logorrhea – Trust me, you're lucky we spared you this one

A revolution is certainly the most authoritarian thing there is; it is an act whereby one part of the population imposes its will upon the other part by means of rifles, bayonets, and cannon, all of which are highly authoritarian means. And the victorious party must maintain its rule by means of the terror which its arms inspire.

– Lenin

LOL – Just as towns replace the natural features for which they were named, internet acronyms supplant the actions they describe

Loyal Opposition – The tacit tolerance existing between two camps that present themselves as opposing poles while maintaining a conspiracy of silence regarding any other options: Democrats and Republicans, terrorists and warmongers, capitalism and communism, marriage and adultery, puritanism and debauchery (*see Head-On Collusion*)

Majority Rule – A ruse to placate an otherwise unruly majority.

The most stable premise for a society based on coercion is to promise power on a rotating basis to whoever can assemble a majority. This gives *everyone* an incentive to maintain that social structure, in hopes that they will get to wield that force themselves one day.

Marginalize – To render peripheral, to *push to the edge*—at which one reaches the threshold of other worlds

Market – The mysterious netherworld in which commodities, having seduced investors and enslaved producers, compete to complete their subjection by

Out on the edge you see all the kinds of things you can't see from the center.

– Kurt Vonnegut

reducing them to consumers. Capitalists are governed by their capital; the economy grants less security and freedom of movement to its human participants than to the objects they consider themselves to possess and control.

In the words of a former addict of heroin, the commodity *par excellence*, "The junk merchant does not sell his product to the consumer, he sells the consumer to his product; he does not upgrade and refine his merchandise, he degrades and simplifies his client."

Marketplace of Ideas – Like human beings, ideas must compete on the uneven terrain of capitalism. Some are backed by academies and media moguls, dollars by the million or billion, entire military-industrial complexes; others are literally born in prison. Of course, despite this, the ones that rise to the top are bound to be the best—just as the human beings who rise to the top of the capitalist economy are clearly superior to the rest.

Hence, in universities, it's taken for granted that people develop ideas and then live according to them, rather than adopting the ones most convenient to their current lifestyle and station. If every idea gets a chance, at least in theory, that proves the merits of the ones that proliferate; it also justifies suppressing attempts to put unpopular ideas into practice (see *Freedom of*

Economy (seated), to Middle Manager:
"More of their blood now, on the double!"

Speech)—didn't they get their chance to compete, like all the others? Meanwhile, ideas that are not concretely demonstrated are rejected as utopian naïveté.

Maroon – To leave someone stranded in an inaccessible place, as on a desert island; alternately, a member of a community of escaped slaves in the West Indies or Americas. The word is derived from the French *marron,* meaning feral. "Whatever you do, don't throw me in that briar patch!"

Marriage – Tying the Gordian knot (*see Divorce*)

Marxism – Why has this single déclassé intellectual, mourned by less than a dozen people at his funeral, become so influential? Perhaps because he offered religious certainty in scientific terms, drawing on the two dominant discourses of our civilization to offset the terrifying unknown always gaping before us. Perhaps because, like every huckster, he took undeniable, heartbreaking, familiar truths as his point of departure, even as he contrived to arrive at the most dubious conclusions. Or is it because—since there is no shortage of men who meet the previous criteria—he became the patron saint of a totalitarian project that ruled half the planet for generations?

Who could avoid forming an opinion on such a personage? The wonder is not that his fame perpetuates itself, but that anyone still subscribes to a cult of personality that has spelled doom from Kronstadt to Pyongyang.* One must be a hardline subscriber to the Great Man theory of history to deny that, were it not for the dictatorships that printed his face on banknotes, we would discuss the subjects associated with him in other language, perhaps with happier results.

Masculinity – Male toughness is so fragile

* To be fair, Marxists suffered from these proletarian victories as much as everyone else; few of the original Bolsheviks made it all the way through the Stalinist purges. The kindest thing you can do for an authoritarian communist is to prevent his Party from taking power, for he is sure to be the next against the wall after you.

Man is least himself when
he talks in his own person.
Give him a mask and he
will tell you the truth.

– Oscar Wilde

Masks – Only by concealing our identities can we shed the masks we have to wear at school, at work, even at home—everywhere there is surveillance, policing, punishment—masks that are increasingly indistinguishable from ourselves

Mass Movement – There is safety in numbers—if you are a number

Mass Production – A social disorder in which objects crowd their makers out of the world, famously depicted in the Disney remake of Goethe's poem "The Sorcerer's Apprentice"

Masterfully – The way a master would—which is to say, well, of course (*see Poorly*)

Materialism – A value system prioritizing material possessions above all else. In certain ideological frameworks, this masquerades as a grand theory of history, complete with a messiah—a revolution brought on by the proper "material conditions"—promising the masses all the possessions they desire.

Me – I am me when I have lost the initiative, just as we are us when we have lost it (*see US*). As for you, it makes no difference whether you have the initiative or not.

Mean Business – Counterintuitively, to be in earnest—business being the one thing about which people are still earnest today

Media – An assemblage of tools with which to expand an audience's conception of what "the world" is to such an extent that their own lives and capabilities seem utterly insignificant; a means of psychological warfare by which people are overloaded with information and desensitized to their own and others' suffering; the sum of all means by which human beings reduce the infinite complexity of reality to a dead-end maze of abstractions—such as the ones in this sentence. So let's try a fable instead:

A team of anthropologists once traveled far across the outback to live alongside an aboriginal group that had experienced little contact with the European settlers. The visitors found their hosts not only peaceable but also welcoming; life among them was for the most part joyous and uncomplicated, and mutual aid was taken for granted as the basis of social relations.

A few months into their stay, the anthropologists received a delivery of additional equipment, including a radio with which they were able to tune in news reports from their civilization. The locals listened with interest, asking for assistance when the newscasters used unfamiliar words. One of the first stories told of a town that had been devastated by a flood.

The entire settlement erupted in activity: bags were packed, tents disassembled, supplies collected. The anthropologists, startled, inquired what was happening. They were answered in the tone one adopts when explaining something obvious to a small child: "We've got to go help those unfortunate people!"

The visitors pleaded with their friends: "But that village is thousands of miles away, across mountains and deserts and wastelands! You could never make it there—and by the time you arrived, if you ever did, the survivors would all be gone and the village with them." At long last, they were able to persuade their hosts to stay put.

This series of events repeated itself over the following days as further news bulletins announced disastrous fires, famines, storms, explosions, massacres, and wars around the world. Each time, the troubled aborigines prepared to break camp and hurry to the assistance of the stricken people; each time, with great difficulty, the anthropologists talked them out of it.

Finally, an entire news program passed without any response, and then another, and another. The anthropologists congratulated themselves: at last they had impressed upon their protégés what it meant to live in a global village. Over the weeks that followed, they noted further changes in their hosts. Many who had been lively and outgoing grew increasingly sullen

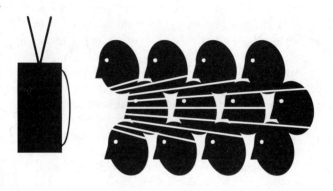

and listless. They sat around, listening to radio reports of calamities from Dover to Peking, rarely lifting a finger to help one another or themselves.

Mediation – Mediated experience is characterized by alienation from the surrounding world and one's own sensory and emotional responses. It can result from using an external intermediary such as a television or the internet, but one might also describe it as an orientation one develops to the world when one is used to experiencing everything through intermediaries.

Picture the first human beings to set foot upon the Galapagos Islands: the unfamiliar plants and animals, the untracked wilderness, the hot sun and salty breeze. Compare their experiences to those of the wealthy tourists that visit the islands today. The latter spend most of each visit inside cruise ships that look like fancy hotels; when they do land on an island, they are only permitted to walk along a strictly designated trail accompanied by a guide who talks constantly at them, framing everything they experience within a standardized narration.* Extend that example to every facet of our lives, and you can begin to understand what mediation means.

* Not to say that bourgeois tourists should be free to run wild across the Galapagos the same way they have rampaged across the rest of the world—on the contrary, the entire world should be free to run wild, so no one has to go halfway across the planet to see a vibrant and unique ecosystem.

This might involve inconveniences for the bourgeois. Studying the colonial history of the Galapagos Islands, it's striking how many strikes, revolts, and riots occurred in the prisons and labor camps there, interrupting the processes of settlement and development. Could it be that the flora and fauna of those fabled isles only survived because of these upheavals? When the history of the world's few remaining green spaces is written, the bulk of the credit for their preservation should not go to wealthy environmentalists but to the workers and inmates who refused, for reasons of their own, to participate in the destruction.

write a story about anarchists!

I'M GLAD I'M
a chilD of
an anarchist
anarchists
or agens the Law
AND Go to
Lots of
MITings

Meetings – Keeping minutes, wasting hours

Megadeath – A unit quantifying the casualties of nuclear war, signifying the deaths of one million people. RAND Corporation strategist Herman Kahn coined this term in 1953 and later utilized it in arguing that nuclear war, far from unthinkable, could be a realistic policy decision for the US government. By the 1980s, the idea that human beings might obliterate themselves by the hundred million had become so utterly mundane that "Megadeth" [sic] came to be better known as the name of a heavy metal band.

Megafauna – Until ten thousand years ago, North and South America were populated by enormous mammals: saber-toothed cats, ankylosaurish glyptodonts, ground sloths twenty feet tall. The Mapinguari, a fearsome beast described in the folklore of various Amazonian indigenous peoples, is presumably one such creature, just as woolly mammoths lingered until a few years ago in a string game played by Inuit children. If even the progeny of the urban middle class tend to be fascinated by stories about dinosaurs and prehistoric mammals, perhaps this indicates that they sense the absence of the animals with whom millions of years of evolution prepared them to share the world.

Megalomania – In common usage, obsession with the exercise of power, especially in the domination of others; in clinical psychology, a pathological condition characterized by delusional fantasies of importance, wealth, or omnipotence; in politics, a combination of the two, with the added complication that the public gives substance to the delusions by sharing them.

Memory – Those who unearth long-lost memories while traveling discover that memory is not so much a static quantity as a dynamic relationship to the past triggered, and framed, by the present. Likewise, one can only reconnect with the heritage of resistance in the process of struggle—as they knew in Odysseus's day, ghosts require a blood sacrifice to take on flesh enough to speak.

Mental Health – Health is the most compelling metaphor with which to impose a normative framework—who wouldn't want to be healthy, or to protect others from being unhealthy?

Mercenary – That is to say, employee

Method Acting – We can only get through our lives by identifying with the characters we are compelled to portray

You're antagonistic to
the idea of being robbed,
exploited, degraded,
humiliated, or deceived.
Misery depresses you.
Ignorance depresses you.
Persecution depresses you.
Violence depresses you.
Slums depress you. Greed
depresses you. Corruption
depresses you. You know,
it wouldn't surprise me if
you're manic-depressive!

– Joseph Heller, *Catch-22*

Microbes – Our only remaining natural predators are the ones too small to exterminate (*see Megafauna*); in place of the risk of being eaten by wolves,* we have the certainty of dying in hospitals

Misanthropy – A sensible conclusion in light of the available data; but people will always surprise you. As William H. Chamberlin detailed in *The Russian Revolution*,

> The mutiny that was to transform the prolonged street demonstrations into a genuine revolution started in the very unit which had inflicted the heaviest losses on the demonstrating crowds… During the night the soldiers discussed their impressions of the day's shooting and agreed they would no longer fire on the crowds.

In a system that brings out the worst in us, it's easy to lose faith in human nature; this is one of the factors that perpetuate the system. But let's not give up on each other—as the saying goes, it's always darkest before the dawn.

Miser – Better own in hell than share in heaven

---

* Milo of Croton, the famed athlete of ancient Greece for whom Paul F. Maul, Jr. is named, was breaking a tree with his bare hands when the trunk snapped back and trapped his fingers in the cleft; he was unable defend himself when wolves set upon him and consumed him. They don't die like that any more.

Everything belonged to him—
but that was a trifle. The thing
was to know what he belonged to.

– Joseph Conrad, *Heart of Darkness*

Misogyny – Pride goeth before a fall

Misrepresent – Represent

Moderation – The one cause for which the bourgeois man is prepared to kill and die

Molotov Cocktail – A message in a bottle

Money – Without it we'd all be rich

Monogamy – An institution that protects romantic partners from learning how to be comfortable with each other's dalliances with others—and usually from learning of them at all

[There is] evidence that the tightness of the pair bond in a species is a fairly reliable indicator of its level of aggressiveness towards its own kind. That figures. If you hate the guts of everybody around you, it becomes absolutely necessary to evolve a system that exempts at least one other individual from your general hostility; otherwise the species would never survive.

– Elaine Morgan,
The Descent of Woman

The Three Stages of Marriage

COURTSHIP

OBLIGATION

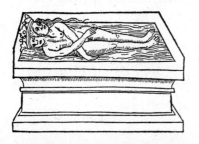

RESIGNATION

Monoglot – It's bad enough to know only one language—how much worse not even to know all of it!

Monotheism – One symptom of paranoia is a tendency to interpret natural phenomena as the workings of an intentional agent

Monument – A device to conceal the past by writing over it.

The Eiffel Tower was completed in 1889, marking the centennial of the French Revolution. Looming over Paris, its grotesque bulk dramatizes a collective denial of the city's bloody history, better characterized by one of the rejected designs for the site: a 300-meter guillotine.

Moral Indignation – Jealousy with a halo

Morale – The deciding factor between passivity and action. Too many would-be revolutionaries underestimate the importance of morale; in fact, it is usually a more important factor than material resources or speculative planning.

Moralism – Right and wrong are superstitions; your desires, however, are real.

Those who cannot achieve their desires, or who despair of doing so, often compensate by constructing imaginary frameworks. For example, if you wish to live in a world in which no one exploits animals, it is moralism to judge those who eat meat *immoral* instead of setting about disabling the animal exploitation industry. People retreat into moralism as a sort of consolation prize, for it is easier to rule in the realm of good and evil, fictitious as it may be, than to come to terms with our limited leverage upon this world and yet persist in endeavoring to change it.

Morality – No forbidding allowed

Mortgage – From *mors,* death; hence, a pledge to trade your life for pieces of paper

Motherfucker – An epithet recalling slave days. If you were a slave, it was likely that the master was sexually assaulting your mother on a regular basis. To call someone in power a motherfucker is to cast light on the genealogical ties that connect those who currently hold power with the brutal history upon which this society was built.

Such a charged word insinuates itself into every context; it becomes an intensifier that can modify anything. Thus many foes of the powerful have become known as *bad motherfuckers*—including the Motherfuckers, short for Up Against the Wall Motherfuckers, the self-professed "street gang with an analysis" that

All the stores will
open up if you will
say the magic words.
The magic words are:
Up against the wall,
motherfucker, this
is a stick up!

– Amiri Baraka,
"Black People!"

sought to push the counterculture of New York City towards armed insurrection at the end of the 1960s.

Motto – No slogans, no watchwords

Movement – A mysterious social phenomenon that aspires to growth yet, when observed, always appears to be in decline.

When social change is gathering momentum, it is protean and thus invisible; only when it stabilizes as a fixed quantity is it possible to affix a label to it, and from that moment on it can only decompose. This explains why movements burst like comets into the public consciousness at the high point of their innovation, followed by a long tail of diminishing returns. A sharper eye can descry the social ferment behind these explosions, perennial and boundless, alternately drawing in new participants and emitting new waves of activity, as if in successive breaths.

Mystic – He goes on and on about the incommunicable

Naïveté – Scrawled by an FBI agent on a photograph of an inexperienced activist: "Suitable for framing"

National Liberation – Make up your mind, it's one or the other

Natural Capitalism – If capitalism were natural, nature would issue its own banknotes

Nature – The term "nature" usually appears in conjunction with its supposed opposite, civilization. This dichotomy implies that the activities and motivating forces of human beings differ categorically from those of other creatures. But once you dispense with the superstition that God created Man in His own image to give him dominion over the fish of the sea and the fowl of the air, it's hard to get around acknowledging that the same natural processes through which stars form and shellfish evolve must also be at work in every aspect of human activity.

All dichotomies are constructs, useful only for what they bring out when used to frame the infinity of existence. If you want to get to the bottom of a dichotomy, you have to begin by asking what it offers those who use it. For capitalists who don't give a damn about ecology, the answer here is obvious: in differentiating nature from civilization, they establish a hierarchy with themselves on top, justifying the exploitation of the aforementioned fish and fowl. Ironically, ecologically-minded anti-capitalists who use this dichotomy may also be unconsciously seeking to establish a hierarchy, but with everything non-human at the top and human beings at the bottom, the sinners cast out of Eden.

This is most obvious in those who anthropomorphize Nature, attributing values and wisdom to it as if it were a sentient being. Some cross the line into authoritarian mysticism, insisting we must adopt those values and abide by that wisdom. This is a ploy, conscious or not, to make their own values and "wisdom" more compelling; nature itself is so infinitely diverse that it would be impossible to distill one lesson or party line from its example† (*see Abstractions*).

Contradictions abound in every normative attempt to define nature. Nature is characterized as that which is "sustainable," as if it were something constant, when in fact the natural world is always in flux. Nature is differentiated from civilization according to vague criteria such as language or domestication, in spite of bees communicating the locations of flowers to each other* and certain ant colonies practicing animal husbandry. Nature is said to have ordained a specific role for every organ in a body and every species in an ecosystem—but these claims are based only on circumstantial evidence. Anyone who believes in

* It would be as impossible for bees to survive without their cultural conventions as it is for human beings to live in snowy regions without the tools we've passed from one generation to the next since before we left Africa. Just like us, the bees *are* their culture—their culture is their nature!—it only appears to be something static and dictated by an autocratic deity ("Mother Nature") because we view it from such a distance. That's trans-species culture shock!

† You want to *live* "according to nature"? O you noble Stoics, what deceptive words these are! Imagine a being like nature, wasteful beyond measure, indifferent beyond measure, without purposes and consideration, without mercy and justice, fertile and desolate and uncertain all at the same time; imagine indifference itself as a power—how *could* you live according to this indifference? Living—is not that precisely wanting to be other than this nature? Is not living estimating, preferring, being unjust, being limited, wanting to be different? And supposing your imperative "live according to nature" meant at bottom as much as "live according to life"—how could you *not* do that? Why make a principle out of what you yourselves are and must be?

In truth the matter is altogether different: while you pretend rapturously to read the canon of your law in nature, you want something opposite, you strange actors and self-deceivers! Your pride wants to impose your morality, your ideal, on nature—even on nature—and incorporate them in her; you demand that she should be nature "according to the Stoics," and you would like all existence to exist only after your own image—as an immense eternal glorification and generalization of Stoicism. For all your love of truth, you have forced yourselves so long, so persistently, so rigidly and hypnotically to see nature the wrong way, namely Stoically, that you are no longer able to see her differently. And some abysmal arrogance finally still inspires you with the insane hope that because you know how to tyrannize yourselves—Stoicism is self-tyranny—nature, too, lets herself be tyrannized: for is not the Stoic—a part of nature?

But this is an ancient eternal story: what formerly happened with the Stoics still happens today, too, as soon as any philosophy begins to believe in itself. It always creates a world in its own image; it cannot do anything otherwise. Philosophy is this tyrannical drive itself.

– Nietzsche, *Beyond Good And Evil*

fixed natural laws or purposes has more in common with the priests who describe sodomy as a "crime against nature" than with the naturalists who have observed homosexual behavior in countless species.

Here is another account of what nature, and humanity as a subset of it, might be. Imagine an infinite, dynamic chaos, in which experiments are ceaselessly taking place. Some of these immediately give way to other experiments; others create feedback loops in which similar processes repeat themselves, changing slowly over time. Within this context, certain members of one species have decided, not surprisingly, that they are special. The traits which they believe differentiate them from other animals—culture, language, free will—are not unique to them, but these appear very different when experienced firsthand than they do observed in others from afar. Most of these creatures can agree that moss tends to grow on certain sides of trees as a result of natural forces, but would exempt their own relationships and decision-making processes from such explanations. If one could ask the moss, it would probably argue that it has free will, too, but prefers the more hospitable side of the tree.

According to this account, everything is natural—from polyurethane to cannibalism, from space travel to breast implants. Free of responsibilities to nature, we can ask ourselves: what do we *want?* Do we desire to replace forests with asphalt and pump

the atmosphere full of carbon monoxide, to supplant reality with virtual reality and ecology with technology? Those who do not wish to need not base their objections upon arguments about what is natural any more than they should base them on superstitious notions of universal morality; they can take their desires as sufficient in themselves to justify action.

But what, a distraught conservationist might ask, are we to make of our species' impending murder-suicide at the expense of all life on earth? Doesn't that imply some kind of essential disjunction between human beings and other life forms?

This can be answered most easily in the form of a parable: Once upon a time, several herds of deer lived in relative symbiosis with the rest of a grassland ecosystem. They would eat the tops of the grass, then move on; the grass would grow back in their wake, fertilized by their manure. One day, a young deer tried eating the roots of the grass as well as the tops; this was natural, as each new generation experimented with new possible food sources. It turned out that the roots were edible, too: suddenly there was twice as much food available within the same area, and as more and more deer adopted this approach, the population of the herd skyrocketed. Other herds began eating the roots as well, so as not to be outdone in the struggle for resources and domination of the gene pool. Only a few marginalized groups retained the earlier custom of eating the tops of the grass and nothing more, and these were driven to the edge of the plain.

After a few decades, almost all the grass had been consumed, and where it had grown only parched desert remained. There were huge numbers of deer by this time, in teeming, oversized herds, looking sleeker and healthier than their ancestors ever had; a year later, their emaciated corpses littered the desert by the million, bones sticking through parched skin. Their rotting flesh contributed nutrients to the scorched desert, and eventually the first shoots of a new crop of grass appeared. As new grasses spread slowly across the desert, a few deer could once again be seen nibbling at them. These were the descendants of the ones who had never begun to eat the roots.

The deer that ate the roots were as natural as any other deer—they were an experiment that worked for a while but could not continue indefinitely. The question is whether we want to follow in their footsteps.

Neutral – For all intents and purposes, dead (*see Neutralized*)

News – A kind of mental weather composed of information.

Every night the overtaxed employees of news networks scramble to distill a few narratives from

"Well, would you look at that! I knew it was dangerous to let all those Mexicans in."

the innumerable events of the day. This would be practically impossible were it not for their biases and the agendas of their employers. One must not look at corporate media reports as "the" events of the day, then, but as strategic maneuvers on the field of public attention (*see Propaganda*). Such broadcasts can still be informative, provided one approaches them as machinations to be decoded: efforts to lay the groundwork for repression, attempts to discredit or distract, admissions of fear and confusion.

To choose a single example—according to our own agenda, of course!—reports of a Swine Flu epidemic originating in Mexico dominated the media throughout 2009. Between 1918 and 1920, a bona fide flu epidemic killed well over 50 million people worldwide, and even today more than 30,000 die of flu-related complications every year in the US alone; Swine Flu, on the other hand, claimed only a few thousand lives worldwide. Fears about looming pandemics notwithstanding, the Swine Flu coverage would be nigh incomprehensible were it not for the implication that immigration from Mexico poses threats that must be controlled. More people have died trying to cross illegally from Mexico into the United States than Swine Flu ever killed; as usual, capitalist treatments are more virulent than the ailments they purport to cure.

Newspeak – Orwell lacked the imagination to see beyond *1984*, when language is not just curtailed, but channeled into formats that preclude meaningful communication in the first place (*see Twitter*)

Nihilism – Boundless faith in the value of nothing and the virtue of destruction. We ourselves, being good nihilists, are agnostics in this regard.

Nihilist – One who has given up hope and belief, without necessarily ceasing to care. Self-professed nihilists typically make a show of wishing to destroy everything and having nothing to lose. Where exactly this "everything" begins and ends is not usually specified: it is one thing to argue that negation is the only meaningful *political* project that is possible today, another entirely to endorse the literal annihilation of the world—an ambitious undertaking at which capitalists and statists excel relative to nihilists.

Pretensions of nihilism frequently correlate with an unsociable individualism and dismissal of collective struggle. Yet the project of destroying everything will demand more widespread participation than the carrying out of mere reforms, seeing as how much of that "everything" is inside us. A misguided nihilist might retort that he wishes to destroy *everyone*, as well: a project more properly described as fascism.

Granted, there are many different strains of nihilism—many different things one can maintain *are nothing,* many different nothings to believe in.

Noble Savage – A myth invented by, and serving the interests of, savage nobles

Nom de Plume – A nom de guerre for one who gambles on the pen rather than the sword.

Mark Twain, Lewis Carroll, George Eliot, George Sand, Anne Rice, Ayn Rand, George Orwell, Isak Dinesen, Joseph Conrad, Pablo Neruda, Tristan Tzara, Yukio Mishima, O. Henry, B. Traven, Dr. Seuss, Voltaire, Saki, Mother Teresa, Vladimir Lenin, Leon Trotsky, Subcomandante Marcos, and practically every MC and DJ in the history of hip hop—if masks were good enough for them, they're good enough for us.

Non-Monogamy – Monogamy doesn't work; polyamory doesn't work; the question is which problems you want to have

Nonviolence – Whether a given action is "nonviolent" is a matter for a Christian concerned about his immortal soul. From a secular perspective, it's more important to ask whether it contributes to or interrupts the violence already in progress.

Nostalgia – It ain't what it used to be

Nouveau Pauvre – The golden fleeced

Nouveau Riche – "Waiter, I've had soup du jour, and *this is no soup du jour!*"

Obedience – On Christmas Eve, 1914, an informal truce broke out between German and British troops

She prefers
them dutiful
and patriotic

stationed across from each other in Belgium. The Germans began by decorating the trees around their trenches with candles, then started singing Christmas carols, notably Silent Night. The British troops responded with English carols, and both sides shouted Christmas greetings across the decimated wasteland that lay between them. A few brave soldiers stuck their heads above the fortifications and, not being fired upon, tentatively made their way forward to meet in the middle of No Man's Land. More followed, and soon the enemy combatants were exchanging gifts—whiskey, jam, cigars, chocolate—and warm embraces.

The surprise truce enabled both sides to recover the bodies of their slaughtered comrades, rotting where they had fallen in No Man's Land. Soldiers of both armies joined in funerals and mourned the dead together. The following day everyone gathered for a football match in the open field; it was a close game, and there was much good cheer and merry-making. We can only imagine what a senseless abomination the war must have seemed to everyone there that afternoon.

By January, the commanding officers had prevailed and the young men who had laughed, sang, cried, and played together a few days earlier were once again shooting, stabbing, and bombing each other.

Objective – Subjective

Occupation – A protracted travesty of justice involving senseless waste of life for the sake of corporate extraction of resources, such as the United States maintains overseas—and you, not coincidentally, experience here at home

Oedipus Complex – According to a certain psychoanalyst, little children want to follow in the footsteps of the Greek hero Oedipus by killing their fathers and fucking their mothers.

Transposed to the political sphere, this theory is often trotted out to suggest that revolutionaries are pathologically mired in adolescence, endlessly rebelling against authority as a representation of the father figure. But there is a precursor of the Oedipus story in which Cronus, having become king of the gods by castrating his father and marrying his sister, devours his children as they are born so they will never replace him. In this earlier narrative, we can see that in fact it is the autocrat who is pathologically frozen in one stage of development, struggling to impose the moment of his power upon eternity. The State is a terrorist attempt to halt time itself—to achieve, in its abettors' words, "the end of history"—by slaughtering those who would inaugurate the world to come; the bullets of the police are *Saturn Devouring His Children*, Goya's terrifying rendition of the Cronus myth, erupting into reality. In this light, the "Oedi-

pus Complex" looks like the paranoid projection of patriarchs seeking to justify their crimes.

Fortunately, if the conclusion of the Cronus myth is any indication, history cannot be held hostage forever.

Ontology – The study of the nature of being. Who says academia is abstract?

Order – Statists justify government on the premise that order is a prerequisite for liberty, but in fact it's the other way around

Outside Agitator – A term of abuse, relying on an unspoken distinction akin to the one Malcolm X drew between the slaves who worked in the slaveholder's house and the ones who worked in the field—albeit viewed from the opposite side of that dividing line. The term is generally used by lapdogs who hope that smearing others will help them to retain their insider status.

Overpopulation – A crisis thought up by Western scientists and intellectuals, perhaps to distract from the more pressing matter that any one of them consumes more resources than a dozen people in so-called overpopulated nations. On the contrary, if there is too many of anyone, it is the Westerners.

Pacifism – Peace at any price

Palinode – A poem in which the poet retracts a view or sentiment expressed in a former poem. Of course, some sentiments make for better poetry than others.

The Dadaist Richard Huelsenbeck, one of the contenders for the title of inventor of nonsense, proclaimed that "Dada is German Bolshevism" and demanded, in its name,

> The international revolutionary union of all creative and intellectual men and women on the basis of radical Communism; the introduction of progressive unemployment through comprehensive mechanization… the immediate expropriation of property (socialization) and the communal feeding of all; further, the erection of cities of light, and gardens which will belong to society as a whole and prepare man for a state of freedom.

That was in 1919, in Berlin, at the crest of a worldwide wave of political and social upheaval. Huelsenbeck

Every time I see peace, you know where I see it? In the cemetery: "Here lies the body of such and such. May he rest in peace . . ." Peace is the diploma you get in the cemetery.

– Peter Tosh

and his cronies urged on the whirlwind with wild whoops and riotous readings of gibberish invoking the death of art and just about everything else.

Yet waves crash and then recede. The cities of light and gardens of Communism were not to be. Wearied by the rigors of being in the world but not of it, Huelsenbeck went back to school in 1922. He eventually settled in the United States, changed his name, broke with his past, and became a psychiatrist. The disciple of disorder who had set out to topple Western civilization now assisted patients in becoming orderly and productive members of society.

Decades later, one of the patients of one Dr. Hulbeck discovered that his psychiatrist was actually Richard Huelsenbeck, Dadaist subversive, and reported him to the FBI. At great expense, Huelsenbeck hired a lawyer, who was ultimately able to deflect this allegation by establishing that the accuser was clinically insane. In his subsequent writings, Huelsenbeck set out to stress the positive and constructive aspects of Dada, reinterpreting it as a step towards Abstract Expressionism; appalled by totalitarian communism and bullied by capitalist democracy, he retreated to merely asserting the rights of the individual.

It's not enough to recant—you have to show that you're willing to participate in the workings of the system, delegitimizing your foes for the deviations you once championed and drafting your own resistance movement into the army of the enemy.

Paranoia – In suspicion we trust

Past – A contested territory obscured by forgetting, which conceals, and remembering, which transforms

Patriarchy – In the workplace, women start out as secretaries and are promoted to lovers; in wedlock, it's the other way around

Patriot – An individual willing to give up freedom without a fight (*see Patriot Act*)

Peace Dividend – Even peace has to pay its own way

Peace Officer – The more law, the less order

Perfume – Air pollution

Perseverance – There's nothing an anarchist can't do

Philanthropist – A capitalist unnerved into returning some of his spoils

Philistines – The illiterati

"And when your comrades are caught?"

             "I'll still have my gun."

"And when you run out of bullets?"

             "I'll pick up a stone."

"What if there are no stones?"

           "I'll have to fight barehanded."

"But what if there is nothing to be
gained by battle?"

             "Then I'll be a conductor,
             like Iannis Xenakis."

"And if you lose your arm?"

             "I'll be a painter,
             like Frida Kahlo."

"But say we take both arms?"

             "I'll become a dancer,
             like Pietro Valpreda."

"And when we take your legs?"

             "I'll be a singer,
             like Victor Jara."

"And when we take your tongue?"

             "I'll be a thinker,
             like Hélène Cixous."

"And when we cut off your head?"

             "Then I'll have been a fighter
             in the resistance."

Plagiarism – Just as those who hold power do not balk at conscription, neither should their foes. Anything they say can and will be used against them.

Popular – Appealing to the lowest common denominator (*see Democratic*). Alternately, a political term meaning "of the people," always hotly contested as to who, exactly, deserves the "the."

This recalls the anti-state communists who, feeling the anarchist movement to be too insular, distanced themselves from it, only to become a subculture within a subculture. There is no returning to The Masses—once your forays into theory have borne you far enough away from them that you can perceive them and the benefits of being among them, the only return is through the process of disillusionment: one must cease to care about motivating The Masses to be reunited with them. Likewise, there is no converting them—no matter how many people come to join you at your outpost, from up close they will never look as impressive as the distant crowd.

Power – A property often conflated with authority. The workers who operate the means of production have power; the bosses who tell them how to use it have authority. The tenants who maintain the building have power; the landlord whose name is on the deed has authority. Armies have power; generals have

"Look around this room—do you notice that you only see the faces of *the people who are here?*"

authority. A hurricane has power; a meteorologist has authority.

There's nothing oppressive about power per se. Many kinds of power can be liberating: the power to provide for those you love, to defend yourself and sort out conflicts, to perform acupuncture and steer a sailboat and swing on a trapeze. There are ways to develop your capacities and capabilities that increase others' freedom as well. Every person who acts to achieve her full potential offers a gift to all.

Authority over others, on the other hand, comes at the price of power over your own life. It is always derived from above: the soldier answers to the general, who answers to the president, who derives his authority from the Constitution. The priest answers to the bishop, the bishop to the pope, the pope to scripture, which derives its authority from God. The police officer answers to chief, who derives authority from the town government, as the judge derives it from the law. The professor derives his authority from the academy, the graduate student derives hers from the text, just as customers derive their authority from the dollar. At the tops of all these pyramids, we don't even find despots—only mere things, specters.

Power Vacuum – "But if we overthrow them without offering something to take their place, what's to stop someone really nasty from filling the power vacuum?"

The mantra of those who are working up the nerve to be really nasty.

Practicality – A fool's virtue, invoked by those with stunted imaginations—or those who have a stake in others' imaginations remaining stunted

Praxis – "Practice," as misspelled by intellectuals to whom it is unfamiliar

Prefiguration – We must be the trouble we wish to see in the world.

Anarchists have long sought to demonstrate the virtues of their vision through prefigurative projects: free food distribution, do-it-yourself health care, collective living arrangements. If only a working model of a better world could be created in microcosm, the thinking goes, everyone who experienced it would become partisans in a revolutionary struggle. Yet in capitalist society, these experiments can only be carried out at the margins: the dregs making the best of debris.

Meanwhile, at the Googleplex, the central organ of the corporation that dominates the world of internet business, cafés staffed by world-famous chefs offer healthy organic food in all-you-can-eat buffets. Google employees drop their children off at free day-care, avail themselves of free hairstylists and laundromats, take

On the big rock candy mountain,
all the snack machines are free

their pets to work, and play Ping-Pong or volleyball on pristine facilities. After they ride in on the free shuttle or park their electrical cars at the charging station, free scooters wait to convey them from one shining example of sustainable architecture to another; they are encouraged to decorate their workspaces however they wish, and whimsical features ornament the campus, including a tyrannosaur skeleton and a rocket ship. Massage therapists remedy their every complaint; a personal lifeguard watches a single swimmer exercising in a swim-in-place pool the size of a bathtub, with different speed settings for water flow. The brightest luminaries in every field are brought in on a daily basis to present free seminars to which everyone is invited—everyone, that is, who manages to produce profit at a rapid enough pace to maintain a foothold in this city on a hill.

If corporations can *prefigure* a world of sharing and abundance more effectively than revolutionaries can, what does that tell us about this strategy? Perhaps that the important thing is not to prefigure utopia—which is already available to the winners of the rat race, albeit intramurally—but rather to prefigure the *offensive* that would render it accessible to all.

Preparation – On April 17, 1974, Ashanti Alston and three friends attempted to liberate the "New York Five"—Jalil Abdul Muntaqim, Albert Nuh

Washington, Herman Bell, and Gabriel and Francisco Torres—who were facing trial for an alleged Black Liberation Army shooting of two New York City police officers at the height of the bloody war on the Black Power movement.

Alston and his friends had been delivering food to the defendants after their court appearances; the visitors were permitted to bring it in a bag, which the guards would search before passing it along. On this day, rather than handing the bag over, they pulled out weapons and locked the guards in the bathroom at gunpoint. Then they hurried to the visiting room and commenced cutting through its metal wall with an acetylene torch. Their comrades urged them on through the visitation windows, along with the other prisoners who had been brought out for visits.

Alston was operating the torch, although he had little experience cutting. The molten metal threatened to seal behind him as he progressed. The other three stood watch, anxiously awaiting the arrival of more guards and the shootout that would follow. Finally, when Alston had cut through all but the last two inches, the flame sputtered and gave out. He had used up the entire oxygen tank and there wasn't another.

As the prisoners on the other side looked on helplessly, the aspiring liberators kicked fruitlessly at the unfinished hole in the metal wall and argued about what to do. In the end, there was nothing for it but to wave ruefully to their friends, beat a hasty retreat, and go underground.

You can never be too prepared, and it isn't always the big things that go awry.

Presumption – Certain pundits have a lot of nerve expostulating against militant action on the grounds that it does not serve the needs of the working class. Those needs are generally a lot more complex and diverse than self-appointed experts assume.

DON'T MAKE ANY PRESUMPTIONS ABOUT WHAT ALIENATES PEOPLE!

REMEMBER, BANK ROBBERS ARE WORKING CLASS, TOO!

Thanassis Papandropoulos had car trouble. His little jalopy had died its final death out in front of his apartment in downtown Athens, and he couldn't afford to have it repaired. If only it had been hit by a bus, or floated off in a flood or something! Year after year, he'd diligently paid the insurance—a sizeable portion of his meager salary—and now all that money had disappeared down the drain.

One afternoon, Thanassis was startled from the football game by the sound of explosions. He hit the mute button and looked out his window. The street was filled with young people, many of them in black hooded sweatshirts, running and shouting. The university was only a few blocks away, so this was not an entirely unfamiliar sight—but this time, they were dragging cars into the middle of the street and setting them on fire.

It only took him a few seconds to realize what he had to do. In a flash, he was down the stairs and out by the curb, fist in the air, shouting "Down with fascism! Avenge Allende!" as he imagined his brother had in '73.

A pair of young toughs approached at a brisk pace, Molotov cocktails in their hands. Thanassis stepped out into the street. "How about this one?" he called out, gesturing at his broken buggy. "Nice kindling, eh?"

The one with the kaffiyeh around his face looked at him incredulously. "Are you kidding? That's a working person's car!"

"Well, it's a car, isn't it? You're burning all the other cars on the block! What about the revolution?"

"Forget it!" hissed the other student, and then, under his breath, "Damn hooligans!" They continued down the street.

"You... you *pacifists!*" Thanassis shouted after them, waving his arms in impotent rage.

"Provocateur!" the one in the kaffiyeh shouted back over his shoulder.

Line after line of rioters passed by him. No one was taking the slightest notice of the jalopy. "Hey!" he cried. "Nice car here! Hey! Over here…" The mob was almost all past. "Hey!"

"Come on, join us!" a beautiful young student urged him, skipping gaily across the paving stones. Thanassis shook his head and scowled: he was an adult with responsibilities and mouths to feed. He couldn't just go gallivanting off whenever he pleased.

A moment later, he was looking at the backs of the last rioters in despair. "Come back here, you cowards! Can't an honest man get his fucking car burned around here? What the fuck is wrong with you people!"

There was nothing for it; he stormed back up the stairs. His wife was still in the kitchen. "What's going on out there, honey?"

"Nothing. Just a bunch of kids." He went to the closet and rummaged around for the fuel they used to power the space heater.

Back on the street, he poured the kerosene all over the hood, then attempted to strike a match from a damp matchbook that had been sitting in the silverware drawer all year. How was this supposed to work, anyway? Damn it—should he have put the fuel *under* the hood?

Just then, a line of armored police came charging up the street—and there was Thanassis, still fumbling with the matches, an empty kerosene can on the curb. He looked up helplessly at the officers rushing forward to apprehend him.

The one in front slammed him back against the hood. "You should be ashamed of yourself—burning a poor man's car like that! And at your age, too! You people are crazy, you're animals—destroying your own neighborhoods! You'll be burning down your own houses next!"

"Leave him be—he must be one of ours," broke in a plainclothes officer, nonchalantly chucking a brick through the window of the flat next door. The policemen continued on at a trot, and Thanassis, dazed, began looking around for the matchbook he had dropped.

He had finally found it and was coaxing the tiny flames to spread when another person came walking up. It was his neighbor, a staunch liberal who had been in the Communist Party in her youth. "What are you doing?" she burst out in dismay. "You too, Thanassi?" He stared back in mute stupefaction. "You know it doesn't do any good! You can't just burn and smash things and expect the world to change—that doesn't do anything for working people! You have to meet people where they're at, with initiatives that provide for their real needs."

Priest – A wolf in shepherd's clothing

Print Media – A verb followed by an object, denoting the archaic practice of printing out text files rather than simply reading them on your computer screen

Priorities – Nikolai Ivanovich Kibalchich, paternal uncle to revolutionary globetrotter Victor Serge, took the side of the poor and downtrodden from an early age. Arrested and tortured by the Tsar's secret police for possessing suspicious literature, he steadfastly refused to inform on his comrades; after his release from prison,* he studied the use of explosives and joined the People's Will, the organization that eventually succeeded in assassinating Tsar Alexander II. The brilliant Kibalchich had been the one to prepare the fatal dynamite.

Kibalchich was swiftly arrested along with the other conspirators. Days later, his lawyer visited him in prison. "You're in a tight spot," the attorney began gravely, setting down a sheaf of documents. "But there could still be hope, if you're willing to—"

* Kibalchich was incarcerated with three fellow radical populists, who were rescued from the prison shortly thereafter by a comrade who worked as a prison guard under an assumed identity until he was able to escort them right out the front gate. The following year, one of the escapees happened upon Kibalchich in a train station; though wanted by the police, he had nodded off and was snoring loudly with a suitcase full of dynamite by his side.

"Forget about me, you fool!" Kibalchich cut in. "Don't you understand? We blew up the *Tsar*! I'm a doomed man! But listen," he confided, "I have something very important to tell you. I've taken advantage of my time here to finalize my plan for a flying machine."

"Get a grip on yourself, man!" pleaded the lawyer. "You still might be able to avoid the death penalty."

Kibalchich would not be swayed. "Time is short," he emphasized, drawing out a piece of folded paper. "I've written out the instructions here, along with a rudimentary diagram. I need you to get these to scientists who can test and develop the idea. This is the last thing I can offer to the people. Promise me you'll do this." And he sat back down in his cell, coolly awaiting death.

One hundred thousand people gathered for the execution, held back by over ten thousand soldiers. On the scaffold, Kibalchich bid his fellows farewell—declining to acknowledge a former comrade who had turned informant—and calmly accepted the hangman's noose.

Almost forty years later, in the tumult of the Russian revolution, Kibalchich's instructions were finally unearthed in the evidence archive of the police. The experts who scrutinized his design were shocked to discover that he had invented the fuel-propelled rocket ship, decades ahead of his time.

A crater is named for him on the dark side of the moon.

Kibalchich's instructions on how to build a flying machine

Private – Pertaining to or characterized by privation.

The word "private" comes to us from the Latin *privatus*, "withdrawn from public life," a use of the past participle of *privare*, "to bereave or deprive," derived from *privus*, "single, individual." This brief etymology speaks volumes about our precious individuality.

Private Property – Better it were neither

Privatize – A word which, tellingly, has no opposite in the capitalist lexicon, "publicize" describing something else entirely

Procrastination – We kill time and it kills us back

Profit – To obtain greater leverage, proportionately speaking, over the goods and services of a society; hence, even if everyone obtained more money at once, we wouldn't all *profit* (*see Inflation*)

Progress – The process of learning from mistakes in order to make graver mistakes.

Industrial technology, for example, far from eradicating all human problems, is now the source of the most pressing ones (see *Genocide*, *Global Warming*, *Iatrogenic*)—but don't worry, all this can be solved with computer technology. Similarly, European refugees brought to the Americas all the afflictions they fled, wreaking even more terrible havoc upon those continents, rather than figuring out how to cure them at home—and some still talk about moving on to space! A child might ask how, if we haven't figured out how to responsibly use the knowledge or resources we currently have, we think we should be trusted with more.

Propaganda – Don't sell bread; share yeast

Property – The thieves had their revenge when Proudhon convicted the bourgeoisie of theft

Property Destruction – A kind of therapy to loosen the unnatural hold certain inanimate objects have on the popular imagination

Prosperity – Don't bother with the stock market index—just count the bums

Protection Racket – A scam in which a gang, institution, or social system offers you protection—for a price, of course—from dangers to which it exposes you (see *Higher Education*, *Insurance*, *National Security*)

Proxy War – In a civil war, rival factions often seek assistance from foreign governments; the latter have agendas of their own, and what might have

"Get off this estate!"

"What for?"

"Because it's mine."

"Where did you get it?"

"From my father."

"Where did he get it?"

"From his father."

"And where did his father get it?"

"He fought for it."

"Well, *we'll fight you for it.*"

appeared a simple local conflict becomes a tangled international intrigue.

Once upon a time, when the governments of different nations generally perceived themselves to have distinct interests, open warfare was relatively common. As individual nations consolidated themselves into blocs held in check by other blocs (see *Mutually Assured Destruction*), proxy war increasingly replaced open conflict. The Cold War between the United States and the Soviet Union, for example, was fought by proxy on battlefields such as Korea, Cuba, Vietnam, Chile, and Nicaragua. In the 1980s, Afghanistan was one of the last of these, and subsequent hostilities between the mujahideen and their one-time sponsors illustrate the hazards of proxy warfare.

One cannot understand the history of resistance without taking into account how many movements and organizations have received foreign aid. For example, after the reunification of East and West Germany in 1990, it came out that the Red Army Faction, West Germany's longest-running armed resistance group, had been funded, equipped, and sheltered by the notoriously repressive East German Stasi, despite the ostensibly conflicting agendas of the RAF and DDR. Likewise, the Serbian group Otpor, known for mobilizing grass-roots resistance to the regime of Slobodan Milošević that culminated in the storming of the capital building and the offices of state television, received millions of dollars from organizations affiliated with the US government. The countless copycat groups that appeared afterwards across Eastern Europe—Georgia's Kmara, Russia's Oborona, Zubr in Belarus, Pora in the Ukraine—could be seen as youth movements struggling against repressive governments or as front groups for foreign powers, depending on your vantage point. Even when they did represent genuine local movements, it was easy for their enemies to portray them as pawns of Western corporate interests.

Since the end of the Cold War, international conflicts are no longer framed in binary terms; instead, they manifest themselves as a global majority attempting to rein in a "rogue state" such as Iraq or North Korea. Rather than openly contending for ascendancy, governments are working together more and more to deepen and fortify the dominion of hierarchical power. Statist and state-sponsored revolutionary struggles are less common than they were forty years ago—in a globalized market, they're too messy and unpredictable to be worth the trouble. It follows that the revolutionaries of the future will probably have to do without government backing.

This is not necessarily for the worse. State sponsorship is a mixed blessing at best, even for those who don't oppose state power on principle. In the Spanish Civil War, a classic example of proxy war, the

Soviet Union backed the communist elements of the Republican forces, while Hitler and Mussolini backed Franco; when Stalin had to appease Hitler to serve Soviet interests, he forced the Spanish communists to sabotage their own revolution, taking down the anarchists and the rest of the Republicans with them. Lacking sponsorship of their own, Spanish anarchists were at a tremendous disadvantage—not so much against the fascists as against their own supposed allies. When the lure of foreign funding no longer exists and all the governments of the world band together to put down uprisings, anarchism will come into its own as the only feasible approach to revolutionary struggle.

Prudence – Better feel once than think twice

Pseudonym – A prudent acknowledgment that the names signed to works have lives of their own apart from those of the authors.

Fernando Pessoa, a Portuguese poet whose alter egoism knew no bounds, wrote as some seventy different personas, each characterized by a distinct personality, style, and relationship to the others—with the effect that when he signed his own name to a text, this too appeared as a persona, a mere artistic convention. This is less apparent in the case of authors who sign only with their own names, but no different. Just as in the fairy tale, while the wizards sleep through the witching hour of the night, their staffs silently slip out to dance in the starlight, so the names and pseudonyms of authors run riot around the world, accruing reputations and associations without regard for the intentions of those who think they possess them.

Elizaveta Ivanovna Dmitrieva was born into a poor family. Tuberculosis killed her father and left her disabled; her sister died in childbirth, and her sister's husband committed suicide shortly thereafter. Despite these challenges, she managed to earn degrees in French literature and medieval history and to secure a humble job at a girls' school.

Dmitrieva had a secret: she was a gifted poet with a powerful imagination. She befriended the influential Symbolist Voloshin, and with his encouragement sent her work to the new journal *Apollon*. When her submissions were rejected—the aristocratic publisher, Makovskii, was not inclined to waste time on schoolteacher's doggerel—she and Voloshin returned to the drawing board.

They invented Cherubina de Gabriak, an exotic young noblewoman raised in a Catholic monastery. Her first letter to Makovskii was written in elegant script on black-edged paper; the envelope was sealed with black wax, stamped with the imprint "Vae Victis!"—*woe to the*

Съ моею царственной мечтой
Одна брожу по всей вселенной,
Съ моимъ презрѣньемъ къ жизни тлѣн-
[ной,
Съ моею горькой красотой.

Царицей призрачнаго трона
Меня поставила судьба...
Вѣнчаетъ гордый выгибъ лба
Червонныхъ косъ моихъ корона.

Но спятъ въ угаснувшихъ вѣкахъ
Всѣ тѣ, кто были бы любимы,
Какъ я, печалію томимы,
Какъ я, одни въ своихъ мечтахъ.

И я умру въ степяхъ чужбины,
Не разомкну заклятый кругъ.
Къ чему такъ нѣжны кисти рукъ,
Такъ тонко имя Черубины?

The poetry of Cherubina de Gabriak
in the journal *Apollon*

vanquished. Reading her poems, in which Cherubina narcissistically—or sapphicly?—reflected upon her own beauty, Makovskii felt he was falling in love.

Soon *Apollon* was dedicating page after page to her work, and all the young aesthetes in St. Petersburg were mooning over her. Dmitrieva spoke with Makovskii via telephone, dropping hints as to where he might find her but always taking care to let the trail go cold. The desperate publisher organized fruitless searches, agonized at the news that Cherubina had fallen ill, and entreated his friend Voloshin to serve as a Cyrano de Bergerac, helping him compose letters and love poetry to the mysterious stranger.

Cherubina was at once the embodiment of the poets' ideal woman and, because she remained out of reach, a ghost who could not disappoint them. But the pressure on Dmitrieva was tremendous. The lines that separated her from her assumed persona were blurring: was Cherubina simply a construct determined by men's desire, or Dmitrieva's real self in another world? She wrote poems to Cherubina, and then wrote poems to Dmitrieva, her double, as Cherubina—longing and fearing to meet, to join her sundered character. In Cherubina's religious visions, Christ looked at her wrathfully—or was it the Antichrist, Christ's own indistinguishable double, beguiling her? Dmitrieva and Cherubina, salvation and damnation: mirrors held up to mirrors, revealing layer upon layer of ambiguity and danger.

Makovskii began receiving letters from an imposter Cherubina; the myth had taken on a life of its own, spinning out of control. Exhausted, Dmitrieva confided in another of the *Apollon* poets, who immediately betrayed her to his colleagues.

Makovskii hastened to meet her, but turned away in contempt from the commoner he found in place of his dream lover. Crushed by rejection, Dmitrieva found that her talents abandoned her. The subsequent revelation of the hoax to the public provoked a major scandal. It was universally assumed that Voloshin had composed the letters and poetry himself, despite his efforts to defend Dmitrieva as the true author.[*]

Years later, banished to Tashkent by the Bolsheviks for her study of anthroposophy, Dmitrieva—now called Vasilieva, on account of marriage—wrote another cycle of poems under another pseudonym.

[*] When Gumilev, another man who had been in love with Cherubina, made a disrespectful comment about Dmitrieva, Voloshin challenged him to a duel—slapping him formally in the face when the staff of *Apollon* had gathered for a group photo in an artist's loft above the Mariinskii theater, where Shaliapin was singing Mephistopheles' part in *Faust*. The two men met at the site of Pushkin's fatal duel and counted out twenty paces before turning to shoot; the four other men present were all poets from rival factions of *Apollon*. Gumilev, an expert sharpshooter, was determined to wash his honor in Voloshin's blood, but miraculously missed; Voloshin's pistol misfired. The two refused to shake hands, hurrying to escape before the police arrived.

Guided by a new amanuensis, a Sinologist, she presented these as the translated works of an exiled Chinese poet, Li Xiang.

Shortly thereafter, Dmitrieva-Cherubina-Vasilieva-Li Xiang died of cancer. As a poet of words, she left behind some compositions; but as a poet of personas, she poses questions to the ages about authorship, femininity, relationships, identity itself.

Public Opinion – The pox populi

Puppet Government – A redundancy. When power itself pulls the strings and competition reigns supreme, no one can determine his own destiny, not even monarchs. As every tyrant learns too late, there are no rulers—only slaves, and free human beings.

Raison d'Etat – As the dictionary explains, "a purely political reason for action on the part of a ruler or government, especially where a departure from openness, justice, or honesty is involved." It's easy to see what sort of reason the state employs—but what is the state's raison d'être?

Rapport de Force – Elected or not, the powerful only take us into consideration to the extent that we can threaten them

Rational – Pertaining to or characterized by rationalization

Rationalize – It appears that the primary function of the frontal lobe is to make excuses for what the rest of the organism is doing. Careful what situations you put yourself in: what you find yourself doing on a daily basis, however arbitrarily, shapes your most fundamental values.

Real Estate – As the economic crisis of 2008 showed, real estate is no more real than any other investment. Property values—like all values—are socially constructed, and may vanish without warning in a crisis of faith.

Reality TV – Once, this would have been a contradiction in terms; today, television is more real than anything we experience in the flesh. If superstars like Madonna must suffer along with everyone else the indignity of not being Madonna, characters on reality TV shows have the strange experience of living in the shadow of their own real lives. To reverse Slavoj Žižek's bon mot that they are still acting on television, only playing themselves, we might say rather that they play their television characters off-screen, too—yet to less acclaim.

Realpolitik – On the contrary, nothing is less inescapably real than politics: they only exist at all on account of our collective pragmatism

Recondite – Abstruse; Delphic; recherché; *obscurum per obscurius**

Only one person ever understood me … and he didn't understand me.

– reputed last words of Georg Wilhelm Friedrich Hegel

* In other words, *ignotum per ignotius*.

Red Herring – An inconsequential issue that distracts from the root of matters; e.g., George W. Bush, carbon offsets, the Green Party (*see also Symptomatic Treatment*)

Reform – Oh yeah, reform—I remember that from reform school!

Reformism – No one is more passionately invested in the system than those who believe it can be improved. For policemen and autocrats, it is a necessary evil, an awkward means to the end of holding power; the oppressed nihilistically accept it as inescapable, if they don't actively oppose it; only the reformer considers it a good in itself—the essential premises must be beyond question, or else his whole project is a mistake. Thus many who set out to right wrongs end up fighting to impose them upon posterity: the judge who began her career as a conservationist sentences the anti-logging saboteur to years in prison.

Likewise, progressives who are not prepared to rule out the possibility that they too might wish to use the apparatus of authority are often loath to push things too far in social struggles, though they may attempt to seize the reins of a movement lest it get out of hand. For example, Gandhi hesitated to lead the peasants of occupied India in refusing to pay rent or taxes—for once they had utilized this tactic against the

A soldier who disobeys an order to fire breaks that oath which he has taken and renders himself guilty of criminal disobedience. I cannot ask officials and soldiers to disobey; for when I am in power I shall in all likelihood make use of the same officials and those same soldiers. If I taught them to disobey I should be afraid that they might do the same when I am in power.

– Mohandas Gandhi, to French journalist Charles Petrasch in *Le Monde*, February 20, 1932, defending his choice not to support the Garhwali soldiers who had refused to fire upon Muslim civilians in Peshawar

British, they might employ it against local landlords and governors as well. This explains the tameness of grassroots movements as well as top-down campaigns: by all means carry signs, *disapprove*—but leave the basic structures intact for when our turn comes around!

Others, the truly incorruptible, may indeed wish to end tyranny and abuse, but feel it to be impossible at the present time; consequently, they hit upon schemes more quixotic than any revolutionism. Petroleum is spurring wars around the globe, so they demand carpool lanes; the polar ice caps are melting, and they aspire to cap emissions. All this, in the name of being *realistic!*

Yet it must be said that the reformist always knows what to do, for he has a simple goal in mind, while the radical who wishes to transform everything never knows where to start. Radicals always find themselves serving as foot soldiers in reformists' crusades; countless reforms, from women's suffrage to the eight-hour workday, have been won with their blood. But whenever radicals stand a chance of upending the whole business, it becomes clear what side reformers are on.

In the third ditch of the eighth circle of hell, Pope Boniface VIII was crammed into a burning pit on top of Pope Nicholas III. Both were stuck upside down, so that Boniface's feet protruded from the top of the hole, where flames licked them continuously. Nicholas, smothering at the bottom, kicked against the other's face, who in turn bit at him and kicked his own feet desperately in the blaze.

From time to time a reformer would come by accompanied by a representative of the management, decrying the harsh conditions and suggesting various improvements. "Is it really necessary that they be upside down?" he'd inquire, standing just out of range of the fumes. "What about a review board? Do they have *any* recourse if they feel mistreated?" His companion listened gravely, nodding from time to time but saying little. Occasionally the reformer grew imploring, wringing his hands: "These are *human beings,* man! Surely you can't be utterly heartless?"

One day, after centuries of this, horned custodians came and pulled out Nicholas and Boniface with pitchforks, then pushed them back into the hole right side up. The reformer was greatly pleased with this; he came around to congratulate Boniface, extending his hand gingerly into the smoke. Of course, the mouth of the pit was still engulfed in flame, so the old pope could only choke and wail while Nicholas gnawed his toes. "We can't do anything about the fire," the reformer explained ruefully, "or else all the other simoniacs will want to know why you get special treatment." On later visits, the reformer commented on the hardships associated with the new arrangement, and eventually the two were returned to their original position.

The popes differed as to the reformer's role and influence. "He means well," Boniface opined between blows from Nicholas's feet; "He just can't do anything for us. His hands are tied by all the bureaucracy down here."

"That's bullshit," Nicholas shouted up in a muffled voice. "Think of Martin Luther, another reformer. Everyone thought he was going to bring about the end of Christianity, but in fact he bought it another five hundred years!" He howled in agony as Boniface sank his filthy teeth into his ankle. "If you ask me, our reformer is higher up than the demons that guard us. Come to think of it, I bet *he's* the one supervising our punishment!"

Regime Change – The details are negotiable, so long as power stays in the hands of a regime (see also *Reform, Red Herring, Symptomatic Treatment*)

Regret – A cheap fee for a costly venture

Religion – Etymologically speaking, "hierarchy" means "rule by the sacred." In theory, religion is not necessarily oppressive; one could hold, as certain revolutionary heretics have, that everyone and ev-

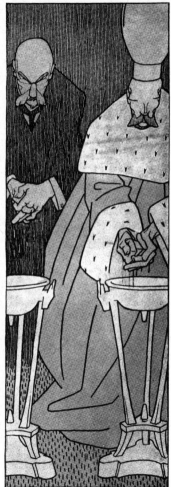

erything is sacred. In practice, the only religions that survived the rise of empires were the ones that were willing to make themselves accomplices to conquest and colonization—not to mention the ones leading the charge.*

Restitution – The notion of reparations still takes for granted the existence of the state that inflicted the original injustice, leaving it intact to inflict further injustices. Seeking compensation legitimizes the idea that there could be a price on suffering, not to mention the authority of the state to bargain for it. Restoring power and self-determination to those from whom they have been taken is not a matter of reparations, but of abolition.

Restorative Justice – On November 30, 1999, during the demonstrations that shut down the meeting of the

* As Jesus explains in the Gospel of Matthew, "Do not think I have come to bring peace on earth; I have not come to bring peace, but a sword. For I have come to set a man against his father, and a daughter against her mother…"

    It's similarly edifying to consult the words of Martin Luther, who appears at first myopic glance to have been a reformer and radical, on the proper treatment of those who resist authority: "Here, let whoever can give blows, strangle, stab—secretly or openly—and remember that nothing can be more poisonous, harmful, and devilish than a revolutionary; just as one must kill a mad dog, for if you do not slay him he will slay you and a whole land with you."

World Trade Organization, a black bloc rampaged through downtown Seattle, smashing the windows of corporate franchises like Niketown and Starbucks. Controversy raged for months afterwards. Who were these anarchists? How dare they damage other people's property? What right had they to trash Seattle?

The story goes that early the following year, the Infernal Noise Brigade, a radical marching band that had participated in the demonstrations, returned downtown. They brought several panes of plate glass with them, which they set up in the center square of the shopping district. Then they distributed fliers explaining that, since the vandalism of the preceding November had apparently caused considerable distress to the law-abiding citizenry of Seattle, anarchists had brought some of their own windows for locals to smash in return as a conciliatory gesture. We can imagine them unsuccessfully attempting to press hammers into the hands of discomfited shoppers until the police arrived. You just can't please some people.

Revenge – Nora Astorga was born into one of the richest ruling families of Nicaragua. Ambitious and gifted, she went to law school; exceptionally intelligent and extraordinarily beautiful, she was pressed with offers of positions in the leading export companies. Instead, she restricted her practice to defending those arrested by the Guardia Nacional of the Somoza dictatorship. The commander in chief of the Guardia Nacional was General Reynaldo Pérez Vega, a key CIA asset. In the prisons and among the resistance, he was known as El Perro, "the Dog": he visited arrested subversives in their cells, smeared their testicles with grease, and released his dogs on them. From time to time, passing Nora Astorga in the corridors of the courts, he murmured to her that if she really wanted to help her clients, she could visit him privately.

One afternoon, upon leaving court, she left word for him that she would be home that night, and if he would like to visit her perhaps he might have what he wished. He came, with his bodyguards, to her home in the center of the city. She opened the door to him herself, clad in a seductive dress, and ushered him into her sitting room where there were flowers and rum and glasses on the table. She laughed as the bodyguards peered suspiciously about the room. She poured him a drink, tasted it, and passed it, laughing, to him. She stood close to him and abruptly kissed him on the mouth. She murmured to him to come into her bedroom and leave the bodyguards outside. Closing her bedroom door behind her, she laughed once more and dropped her dress to the floor. He embraced her and she pressed up against him, pressing her laughter into his mouth, holding his head tight as the Sandinista slipped out of the closet and cut his throat.

Incredibly, she managed to climb out a window and escape from Managua to join the guerrillas in the hills. She had to leave her children sleeping in their beds. When, three years later, the Sandinistas entered Managua in triumph, she was made justice minister, and decreed the abolition of the death penalty.*

Review – Those who can, write; those who can't, write reviews. Writing reviews is the surest shortcut to a sensation of power for those who lack the dedication necessary to create something of actual worth. In passing judgment on others' work, the reviewer experiences a fleeting high of self-importance cheaper than any other.

* Let no one mistake this heartening anecdote for an endorsement of the state. We won't know state torture and murder are gone for good until every last government has been overthrown.

"O that mine enemy had written
A book!"—cried Job: —a fearful curse.
– Percy Bysshe Shelley,
quoting Job 31:35 in the
King James version of the Bible

The Fine Art of Coarse Criticism:
A How-To Guide

Deceptively simple and mundane, reviews are often
assumed to be easy to pen; in fact, it's almost impossible to compose one worth reading. Fortunately for
the next generation of hacks, after squandering the
best years of our writing careers composing purple
prose for the throwaway tabloids of yellow journalism, we've perfected this most elusive of literary
forms. To save you and your potential readers the
trouble of suffering through this learning process,

we present here a surefire failsafe handy guide to the most rightly unappreciated literary form of the 20th century. Mix yourself a stiff metaphor, cultivate an air of supercilious indifference—a prerequisite for any reviewer worth the salt he hopes to pour in others' wounds—and read on.

The Comparison

This is the most common convention in the reviewer's repertoire, and the most swiftly, thoughtlessly trotted out. It comes in three basic varieties:

A is like B: *"Oscar Wilde's* The Picture of Dorian Gray *is basically a rewrite of Goethe's* Faust, *right down to the use of punctuation marks." "Like any other band with guitars, bass, and drums, Cannibal Corpse owes everything to Chuck Berry."*

A is like B + C: *"The sequel to* The Matrix *is the bastard child of Nintendo video games and MTV's 'The Daily Grind.'" "Dragonforce sounds like Richard Marx with double bass."*

A is like B (perhaps + C) under aggravating conditions: these can include, for example, drugs—*"Jackson Pollock is like, uh, Matisse on serious methamphetamines"*—violence—*"Baudrillard offers the sort of insights Foucault would have hit upon if he'd suffered severe head trauma at an early age"*—evocative locations—*"Imagine Tolstoy's War and Peace if it were set in a Soviet gulag across only three days; there you have it, Solzenhitsyn's The First Circle"*—or, for maximum cliché action, all three: *"Muppet Burger's new album "Fuzzy Massacre" sounds like Sun Ra and Sinead O'Conner, cranked out of their heads on cough syrup and banana peel blunts, beating the stuffing out of Morrissey in a dark alley while humming La Marseillaise to themselves."*

The Fawning Accolade

As a general principle, a critic should not tender a positive review unless he stands to gain in some way, lest he sully the bad name of the profession. Yet demonstrating one's superiority by exhibiting prescient taste can be as gratifying as the more direct approach of simply declaring something inferior. Of course, the power dynamics shift as soon as the spotlighted upstart gains a certain amount of attention: then, glorification accrues to the artist rather than the reviewer, so one must return to scorn and ridicule.

Things are not usually even this complex: a guest list and bar tab beckon, a senior editor threatens, advertising dollars await, Public Opinion counsels that this going to be a Hot Item this year and those who fail to get on board do so at their own peril. One must give positive reviews to *something,* after all, and it never hurts to kill two birds with one stone.

Sometimes it happens that a neophyte, carried away by actual passion unbecoming of the serious journalist, expresses honest appreciation. Please, resist this temptation. Everyone has mouths to feed in this business, and a certain professional standard of restraint and objectivity is only common sense.

The Interpretation

The critic does well to cast himself as the artist's interpreter, a modern-day successor of the priests who explicated the drugged ravings of the Oracle of Delphi. This relationship places the critic in the more essential role: any damn fool can get hooked on heroin and put a few chords together, but it takes a Greil Marcus to construct meaning out of the resulting cacophony and trace its lineage back to the Anabaptists. Artists are idiot savants who achieve greatness by unhinging themselves, as Rimbaud himself insisted—that's why the best of them die young. Does it make sense to allow such people to speak for themselves?

For best results, select the most incoherent and opaque artwork, rewarding artists and movements that produce this with positive coverage. Ideally, the public, knowing themselves unqualified to do, feel, or think anything on their own, should bypass the artwork completely, coming directly to the critics. It goes without saying that any creative person who makes concrete statements—the musician who speaks between songs, the poet who writes about the war—should be decisively ignored, or at least dismissed as superficial. This policy worked fabulously for art critics throughout the 20th century, and indeed may explain the evolutionary trajectory of Western art across that era.

The Personal Anecdote

When a reviewer feels the itch to hold forth about his own extensive experience as a widely traveled citizen of the world, he need not stick to the matter at hand. Many a frustrated travel writer, philosopher, religious mystic, and misanthrope has found a lasting career as a reviewer—not least because it is one of the few writing jobs in which it is not important that anyone read your work.

Hearsay and Speculation

Reviewers have to worry about their facts being checked about as much as federal agents at a bail hearing. Any old thing you heard or might have heard is fair game. It's your job to keep things interesting, so don't hesitate to spice up your review with a little scandalous gossip: *I used to be a card-carrying member of The Anarchist Movement, until I heard Bakunin was actually a paid agent of the Tsar.*

The Stream of Invective

This can range from a simple insult (regarding Jack Kerouac's claim that he wrote *On the Road* in a matter of days, Truman Capote quipped, *"That's not writing, that's typing"*) to a veritable torrent of abuse—which may, after all, be well deserved:

> Imagine Def Leppard if Wesley Willis was the principle songwriter and their vocalist sounded like a character from The Flintstones. Now imagine whatever you just imagined, only worse. There you have it, the debut album from Andrew WK, "I Get Wet." This makes the stuff they play over the public address systems at professional football games seem bookish and highbrow. The lyrics are pathologically tautological ("you can't stop what you can't end"), the riffs sound like cheap radio advertising jingles with some of the notes played wrong, the end of every song sounds like a television being switched off. My friend Gabe says this makes him feel like he's at a keg party at a frat house, but there are no women there, just drunk, belligerent jocks and brain-damaged football players wrestling the furniture and shouting each other down about the stock market.

Myself, I can't help but imagine this blaring over the speakers in the personnel bay of an army helicopter as GIs are airlifted into an Iraqi village to slaughter mothers and children—and as if in anticipation of this, Andrew has recorded a track in which he bawls over and over "You better get ready to kill, get ready to die." Even if you didn't have serious doubts about the future of Western civilization before you heard this release, one listen will make you a revolutionary in the tradition of the Dadaists and Situationists who set out to put an end to art itself—if it doesn't reduce you to utter despair.

Absurd Allegations

When it's not possible to unleash a well-founded Stream of Invective, but the reviewer still desires to maintain the readers' attention, he falls back upon what philosophers call the straw-man argument: he concocts a ludicrous effigy of the subject of the review and displays his great prowess by painstakingly tearing it apart.

In ideological circles—including certain anarchist camps, strange to tell, where so much talk of solidarity would lead one to expect constructive criticism to be the order of the day—this approach is even more common than the Comparison. Those who believe—often correctly—that their ideas can only be of interest if all other ideas are entirely bankrupt must remain ever vigilant, ready to pounce upon and discredit other thinkers by any and every means.

The Irrelevant Digression

The digression is a sort of verbal smoking break in which the writer gets up from his desk, takes a breath, and stretches his legs, all without ceasing to address the reader. Reviewers who wish to curry favor with discriminating readers should throw in as many of these as possible: the less attention they pay to the subject of the review, the more bearable their writing is bound to be.

Sample Exercise

Dash off a review of this book and upload it posthaste to the World Wide Web. Whether you compose a Stream of Invective, an Absurd Allegation, or an Irrelevant Digression, and regardless of whether you have ever undertaken to write a single word before in the English language—or have read any of this book besides than this sentence—your review is sure to be more balanced and informative than the work of *professional reviewers*.

Revolution – War without enemies

Revolutionary Struggle – A conflict pitting an enter-prising minority against all who hold power, all who obey orders, all who do nothing, and all who wish to resist but don't know how to or else lack the courage

Revolutionary Subject – Talk long enough with someone whose thinking has been molded by Marx-ism, and you may hear about an elusive personage known as the revolutionary subject: "But who are you proposing as the revolutionary subject, if not The Workers?" "Perhaps housewives are oppressed, but as they lack access to the means of production, they cannot be a revolutionary subject."

According to the Marxist tradition, the proletariat—those who have nothing to sell but their labor, who accept wage slavery for fear of starvation (*see Disincentive*)—will rise up, seize control of their workplaces, and use them to produce a paradise where all is held in common. As the 19th century recedes further and further into the smoke of failed revolutions, this story grows less and less convincing. An ever-growing proportion of human beings have nothing to do with the means of production proper, and many of us have serious misgivings about whether capitalist technology can produce anything worth having in the first place. What are the kids who work part-time at the pretzel

stall in the mall supposed to do with their workplace? Does a rainforest count as a means of production—and *should* it? Blithe assurances aside, how can we be sure this will put an end to patriarchy, white supremacy, animal exploitation, and global warming?

These are all non-issues for the traditional Marxist. The notion of the revolutionary subject is premised upon two "the"s: *the* revolution, and *the* subject that brings it about. As Marxism privileges economics over all other ways of interpreting the world, both revolution and revolutionaries must be economic in nature; any other considerations are bourgeois hogwash.*

Anarchists believe that hierarchy has no one essential form, and therefore recognize multiple legitimate fields for resistance. An anarchist conception of the "revolutionary subject" would have to include all

---

* Speaking of bourgeois hogwash—at the risk of fatally boring anyone without an academic interest in philosophy, let's compare the revolutionary subject with the subject of René Descartes' *cogito ergo sum*. Descartes unthinkingly premised his famous formulation on the grammatical rules of his language: a verb presupposes a subject—so if thinking is taking place, the great I of the philosopher must exist. It seems many Marxists do the same thing: "There's going to be a revolution—that much we know from the Scriptures—ergo some class that exists today must be the ones who will make it, i.e., the Revolutionary Subject." A rival philosopher once countered Descartes' argumentation by asserting that some verbs demand no subjects: for example, "It's raining." Similarly, could we imagine a revolution that *makes revolutionaries* of the participants, rather than vice versa?

individuals and demographics to the extent to which they contest domination.† In contrast to Marxist dogma, let us propose that the determinant matter in this struggle is not *access to the means of production* but *capacity to interrupt the processes that maintain hierarchy*, which are as broadly distributed as hierarchy itself. Unemployed slum-dwellers can block highways that supply factories; survivors of domestic violence can maintain safe houses and confront perpetrators; vandals and hackers can seize walls and websites for communication; folk artists can undermine the processes of projection and identification that cause people to conflate their rulers' interests with their own. All of this counts towards revolution.

At worst, the notion of a single revolutionary subject fosters a determinism that objectifies human beings and revolutionary struggle while avoiding the complexities of reality. What are the workers doing? When will they finally be ready to revolt? What are we supposed to do in the meantime? Likewise, fixation on the working class can promote a sort of class-based identity politics—even though class is not an identity, but a relationship. Growing up poor doesn't give anyone the right to be Joseph Stalin. Anybody who

† Obviously, different classes tend to have different degrees of motivation to resist hierarchy, according to the privileges they receive in the current state of affairs. But let no one say it is ever actually in anyone's best interest to oppress others.

wants to change the subject back to the proletariat once the issue of domination itself has been broached is not a comrade.

To sum up: ask not who is the revolutionary subject, but how you can become one.

Rhetoric – A means of conveying listeners from one position to another via a sort of hot-air balloon

Robbery – Legend has it that one night Voltaire and some traveling companions lodged in a wayside inn. The surroundings were evocative, and after supper they agreed to take turns telling robber stories. When Voltaire's turn came, he began: "Once there was a high-ranking employee of the Internal Revenue Service." He stopped there, and his companions encouraged him to go on. "That," he said, "is the story."

Romance – An airborne STI. Symptoms include increased sensitivity to sight, sound, and taste; decreased vulnerability to sleep deprivation and the elements; and general delirium, which in extreme cases can precipitate a complete reevaluation of priorities. Like all STIs, new outbreaks are feared by those in both monogamous and polyamorous relationships, and associated with all sorts of threatening possibilities. In bourgeois circles, this fear has been expanded into a religious creed characterized by a general suspicion

Whoever knows he is deep, strives for clarity; whoever would like to appear deep to the crowd, strives for obscurity.

– Friedrich Nietzsche,
The Gay Science

of all intense or transformative experiences: stick to bland foods, sleep dreamlessly, and stay out of the rain.

Rorschach Test – Although astrology has been scientifically discredited, it persists because it offers a frame, however arbitrary, through which to interpret the vast and otherwise opaque expanse of our lives. It is not the stars that tell us about ourselves, but our very interpreting.

One might say the same thing about other fields, including the "hard" sciences. If Herbert Spencer could see survival of the fittest as the most determinant factor in evolution while Peter Kropotkin interpreted the same raw material in terms of mutual aid, perhaps scientific theories tell as much about the class commitments of their authors as they do about the natural world.

Rule – Democracy, bureaucracy, autocracy, aristocracy, plutocracy, technocracy. Each of these words describes government by some subset of society, but they all share a common suffix, implying a common form, a common logic.

All of them are derived from *Kratia*, rule—associated with Kratos, the classical Greek deity representing force. For the ancient Greeks, every abstract concept was personified by a divine being; the kind of power that is wielded over others was embodied in this implacable Titan.

ARISTO
AUTO
BUREAU
DEMO
PLUTO
TECHNO
CRACY

One of the oldest sources on the subject opens with Kratos forcibly escorting the shackled Prometheus. Prometheus is being punished for stealing fire from the gods to give to humanity, the quintessential act of selfless insubordination. Kratos appears as a ruthless jailer, unquestioningly carrying out Zeus's order to chain the rebel Titan at the end of the earth. Even Kratos's fellow jailer Hephaestus denounces him: *"You were made for any tyrant's acts."**

Kratos can bind Prometheus, punishing and suppressing the creative impulse, but he cannot free him, nor can he give *fire* to humanity. This is what autocracy and democracy have in common, what links all systems of government: in establishing *power over,* they can only hobble their subjects, never ennoble them. The institutions of coercion—the legal apparatus, police, and military, which have changed little in all the transitions from feudalism to capitalist democracy—are made to impose tyranny, whether the tyrant is a king, a class of bureaucrats, or the people themselves.

Sacred – Possessing a quality characteristic of cows, venerated by the cowed

* Aeschylus's millennia-old play, *Prometheus Bound*, translated by Percy Shelley and Thomas Medwin. In Shelley's follow-up, *Prometheus Unbound*, the tyrant who had Prometheus chained is overthrown by Demogorgon—an allegorical figure Shelley uses to represent the people, *demos*, not in league with Kratos as in *democracy*, but rather as *Gorgon*, a monster.

The reason Milton wrote in fetters when he wrote of Angels & God, and at liberty when of Devils & Hell, is because he was a true Poet and of the Devil's party without knowing it.

– William Blake

Salary – The wages of sin is death; the wages of the bourgeois are—salaries (*see Installment Plan*)

Samizdat – The production of literature banned by the former communist governments of eastern Europe; the term is a play on Gosizdat, the Soviet state press, and translates to "self-publishing." Throughout the greater part of the twentieth century, the best literature, philosophy, and history in the Soviet Union was copied by photo-reproduction and distributed through underground channels—as it is in the United States today.

Satire – Sad ire

Schizophrenia – A long-term mental disorder involving a breakdown in the relation between thought, emotion, and behavior, leading to faulty perception, inappropriate actions and feelings, withdrawal from reality and personal relationships into fantasy and delusion, and a sense of mental fragmentation. When this takes place all at once throughout a society, it is no longer discerned as a disorder, but on the contrary lauded as "good citizenship," "patriotism," "hard-nosed pragmatism."

Scientific Method – Formulate a question; compose a hypothesis; make a prediction based on it; test your

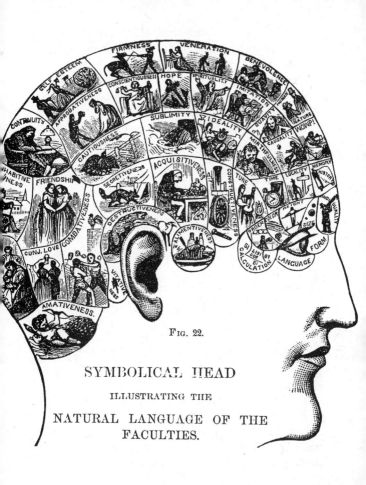

FIG. 22.

SYMBOLICAL HEAD

ILLUSTRATING THE

NATURAL LANGUAGE OF THE
FACULTIES.

prediction under controlled conditions; analyze the results. There you have it, the method responsible for the rapid progress of technology over the past few centuries.

In theory, this should produce an ever-expanding pool of universally applicable knowledge. In practice, it's not so simple, even before you get to copyright issues. Anyone who has applied for employment as a guinea pig in a corporate medical study knows that neither the ones who direct the inquiries nor the unfortunates who rent out their bodies are disinterested seekers of truth. Not even the hyper-rationalism that gave rise to it is compatible with pure capitalism.

Screen – A surface onto which pictures and movies are projected, or upon which data and images are displayed, e.g., on a television set, computer monitor, or phone; alternately, as it happens, a device to block or conceal

Scripture – That which the devil quotes for his purposes

Seed Corn – The corn from which the following year's crop is to be grown. Every relationship can withstand a certain amount of stress; but when you demand more from a friendship or love affair than can it can replenish on its own, you are eating the seed corn.

Self-Determination – All the money in the world can't buy it

Self-Management – The lunatics are running the asylum—it hasn't yet occurred to them to *leave it*

Semantics – The science of evading the point

Servility – A means of gaining the element of surprise

Shopping – When the entire world is held hostage, one can't help wishing to regain one's rights to it, even if that means buying them back piecemeal

Skyline – A three-dimensional bar graph displaying the property values in an urban area

Slogan – A pithy formulation for mobilizing unre-flective masses; as every politician and advertising executive knows, the less a statement means, the more people can rally behind it.

Some peoples imagine their dead, or certain of them, as fighting hosts. The Celts of the Scottish Highlands had a special word for the host of the dead: *sluagh*, meaning "spirit-multitude." To quote one commentator: "The spirits fly about in great crowds like starlings, up and down the face of the world, and come back to the scenes of their earthly transgressions. They fight battles in the air as men do on the earth. They may be heard and seen on clear, frosty nights, advancing and retreating, retreating and advancing against one another." The word *gairm* meant shout or cry; *sluagh-ghairm* was the battle-cry of the dead.

This later became "slogan." The expression we use for the battle cries of our modern crowds derives from the Highland hosts of the dead.

Smart Bomb – A dumb idea

Social Media – A Distributed Denial of Service attack on your brain

Social War – A civil war is a conflict between citizens of the same nation; in this regard, civil war is ongoing wherever capitalism, patriarchy, and white supremacy prevail, reinforced by the institutions of the state itself. In some places, this is subtle; elsewhere, such as the Deep South, it's easy to see that the Civil War never ended.

Social war is something else. Historically, the term is used to describe wars between allies, starting with a struggle that pitted ancient Athens against several of its confederates.

During the youth of Julius Caesar, several of Rome's Italian allies revolted to protest being treated as inferiors to the capital. After four bloody years, Rome quelled this Social War by extending full rights of citizenship to all the Italians that did not revolt. This was an important step in the evolution of national identity: it ceased to be a matter of lineage or residence and became an abstract category in which ever more people could be included—provided they gave up their previous combative allegiances. If not for this, Rome could never have become a continent-spanning leviathan in which German and Arab generals presided over the subjugation of their own peoples.

Recently, some insurrectionists have used the expression "social war" to describe taking a side in a society at war with itself, seeing this as an improvement on the narrow and outdated notion of class war. But the previous history of the term haunts us. Are we just rebellious confederates of the empire, ready to affirm *social peace* as soon as we're granted more inclusion? Do we fight for better standing—for everyone to have the right to be a good citizen—or to abolish standing and citizenship altogether, along with *rights* and *goodness?* Perhaps what we want is neither civil war nor social war, but something that renders both obsolete.

Socialist Realism – A contradiction in terms

Soft Drink – Worthless things make the best commodities, as their prices are indisputable

Specialization – One day, a group of villagers paid a visit to her hut. They sat down on the grass mats on the floor, and one of them addressed her: "Ever since you came here, you have been asking us a lot of questions. Now we would like to ask you a question."

One of them picked up the drinking glass, one of the few relics of her civilization she had brought with her. "Please," he began, politely, "how do you make this?"

"Oh yes, well," she stumbled, trying to collect the right words in their dialect to explain the process, "it's quite simple, really. You take sand and you heat it with fire, and then you mold the glass."

"Aha!" the villagers responded, enthusiastically nodding their heads as they passed the glass around their circle. "Tomorrow, after breakfast, we will meet on the beach, and you can show us how to do this ourselves."

Her hosts understood none of the jumbled, incoherent protestations that followed. They did, however, understand her refusal. Thereafter, they let it be known throughout the village that the real reason for the anthropologist's presence among them had been revealed: she had been sent because she was an incompetent, incapable of the simplest crafts of her culture.

Stalinism – Not a consistent ideology, but a contradictory aggregate of all the positions that could be inferred from Stalin's actions at various points in his career. One can't help but pity the toadies of the Comintern, who had to play along at the risk of losing their heads as the correct lines on fascism, internationalism, and everything else changed according to what was politically expedient for the Dictator of the Proletariat. That a few psychopaths persist in this today, when the beloved leader is long dead and there are no rewards for doing so, boggles the mind.

Status – A measure of worth independent of personal qualities, treatment of one's fellows, or capacity for self-determination, conveying only how much power one has over others. In the death camps during the Holocaust, Victor Frankl heard a fellow prisoner say of a "capo" (a prisoner given life-and-death control over other prisoners by the Nazis): "Imagine! I knew that man when he was only the president of a large bank. Isn't it fortunate how far he has risen in the world?"

Stockholm Syndrome – On August 23, 1973, Jan Olsson, a repeat offender on leave from prison, walked into *Kreditbanken* in central Stockholm and attempted a hold up. The police were called immediately, and two officers entered the building. Olsson opened fire, injuring one policeman; he ordered the other to sit in a chair and sing, and the cowed Swede attempted a rendition of "Lonesome Cowboy." Altogether, Olsson managed to take four hostages; in return for their safety, he demanded that his friend Clark Olofsson be brought to the bank, along with three million Swedish Kronor, two guns and bulletproof vests, and a fast car.

The government acquiesced, bringing in Olofsson and promising a car to come; Olsson and Olofsson barricaded themselves and their hostages in the inner vault of the bank. In discussion with Swedish Prime Minister Olof Palme, Olsson said he would kill the hostages if his demands weren't granted in full. Despite this, another hostage, Kristin Enmark, said she felt safe with her kidnappers but feared that the police might escalate the situation.

The following day, Prime Minister Palme received another call. This time it was Kristin Enmark, who said she was very displeased with his attitude and asked him to let the robbers and hostages leave.

Olsson emphasized his readiness to kill the hostages if the government attempted a gas attack; Olofsson passed the hours pacing the vault, singing Roberta Flack's "Killing Me Softly." On the fifth day, the government hazarded a gas attack anyway, and Olsson and Olofsson surrendered without harming anyone.

Both Olsson and Olofsson were sentenced to extended prison terms. However, Olofsson successfully appealed his conviction on the grounds that he had only joined Olsson to keep the situation calm, and returned to his criminal career. He later met former hostage Kristin Enmark several times, and their families became friends.

Olsson spent several years in prison, where he received many admiring letters from women. Upon his release, he resumed illegal activity, eventually going underground to escape further prosecution.

He reappeared in 2006, traveling to Sweden from Thailand after almost a decade and a half on the run. He went to a Helsingborg police station to turn himself in, hoping to come clean and turn over a new leaf. The first police officer he spoke to, however, urged him to leave the premises: "Take off, Janne, you're wanted." Olsson refused to leave and insisted on making a full confession. Finally, an official sat down with him and brought up his file, only to discover that the prosecutor had dropped his charges.

Upon leaving the police station, Olsson proceeded directly to the nearby tax office, where he filed his paperwork and arranged to begin receiving the pension due every Swedish senior citizen.

At first glance, this story is simply a charming idyll demonstrating the permissiveness of the Swedish welfare state. Can you imagine mere bank robbers getting a direct line to the President of the USA? But there's another layer: the expression "Stockholm Syndrome," coined by the psychiatrist who assisted police during the robbery, has entered common parlance to describe the phenomenon of hostages associating their own interests with those of their captors.

This phenomenon is already painfully familiar to many of us, as survivors often maintain loyalty to loved ones who perpetrate physical and emotional abuse. One might say it is both to our credit and to our misfortune that human beings tend to develop emotional ties to those around us, however monstrous they are.

Alternately, one can see Stockholm Syndrome as evidence that people tend to identify with the most powerful individuals in a situation, even when the interests of those individuals conflict with their own. Perhaps they do this in order to avoid coming to terms with their subjection; perhaps there is something seductive about domination itself. We can see Stockholm Syndrome grown to epidemic proportions in the patriots and party faithful who idealize their rulers while the latter loot all their resources, decimate the natural environment, and provoke terrorist attacks against them.

The most famous poster child for Stockholm Syndrome was millionaire heiress Patty Hearst, who was kidnapped by the Symbionese Liberation Army in February 1974 only to resurface in April as an active participant in an SLA bank robbery.* She participated in SLA activities until her arrest in September 1975, even after the police had murdered most of her compatriots; upon being booked into prison, she listed her occupation as "urban guerrilla." When her trial commenced the following year, her lawyer argued that she had been brainwashed and coerced, making the most of the recent entry of Stockholm Syndrome into the public imagination. President Jimmy Carter commuted her sentence after only three years, showing that spoiled rich girls can get away with whatever they want—even attempting to overthrow the government. Patty went on to win aristocratic kennel club competitions while her comrades from the SLA rotted in prisons and coffins, thanks in part to her turning state's evidence against them.

Self-serving recantations notwithstanding, Hearst's conversion and Kristin Enmark's harsh words to the

* In return for her release, the SLA demanded that the Hearst family distribute $70 worth of food to every needy Californian, which would have cost an estimated $400 million. Hearst's miserly father distributed only a few million dollars worth of food in the Bay Area, and the SLA refused to release Hearst on the grounds that the food was of poor quality. In a recording subsequently released to the press, Hearst commented that her father could have done better. Be that as it may—while we can't countenance the SLA's wanton disregard for human life, let no one say armed struggle never provided for the hungry.

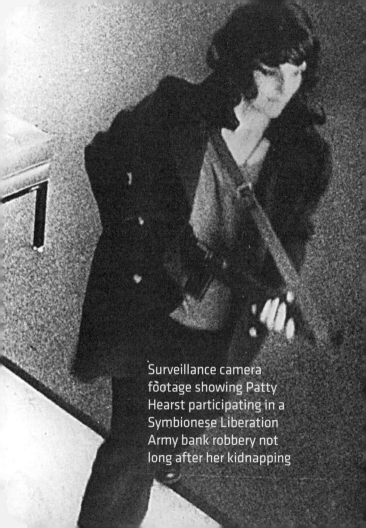

Surveillance camera footage showing Patty Hearst participating in a Symbionese Liberation Army bank robbery not long after her kidnapping

Swedish prime minister suggest a third interpretation of the cause of Stockholm Syndrome. Might it be that kidnappers, however domineering and dangerous, appear downright cuddly in contrast to the impersonal brutality of the State? For the duration of their confinement, hostages experience reality from the vantage point of the hunted, rather than the hunters. In Hearst's case, that experience was compelling enough to last until the authorities forcefully relocated her to a space in which they could dictate reality entirely on their terms. So when was Hearst really brainwashed—when she was kidnapped by urban guerillas, or when the state kidnapped her back? Or when she was born and bred into a society in which it is taken for granted that some people are millionaire heiresses while millions more inherit nothing but poverty and oppression?

Strategy – Repeat after me: *goals, strategy, tactics.* Identify your goals; hammer out a strategy to achieve them; utilize tactics that advance that strategy. All too often, activists begin from the opposite direction, adopting by default whatever strategy enables them to employ their favorite tactics. Indeed, as action is more contagious than analysis, this tendency is very difficult to avoid.

On the other hand, certain tactics have a great deal of ideology encoded into them, and this can be a virtue. Smashing windows can express a rejection of property rights, but it is unlikely to advance an electoral campaign. It follows that apparent disagreements about tactics or strategy often hide real conflicts over goals. Those who think it is more important to maintain the allegiance of the middle class than to make common cause with the disorderly and dispossessed probably don't want to abolish capitalism and the inequalities it causes, whatever they profess.

Style – Among the upper ranks of the bourgeoisie, the police are rarely seen, but fashion carries a gun

Substitutionist – Some Marxists use the expression "substitutionist" to allege that a group is prioritizing its own activity over the activity of the proletariat as a whole. This criticism can be leveled fairly at authoritarian groups of all stripes, but—originating as it does in an authoritarian camp—it is often directed instead at those who wish to proceed directly to struggle without waiting for advice or unanimity.

One might counter that it is equally misguided to substitute the initiative of the proletariat or any other abstract body (*see Imaginary Friend*) for one's own initiative, which must necessarily comprise a part of that whole. It is only in moving directly to action that we can find others who wish to act, with whom to set contagious examples of revolt.

These methods lead, as we shall see, to the Party organization "substituting" itself for the Party, to the Central Committee substituting itself for the Party organization, and finally to the dictator substituting himself for the Central Committee.

– Leon Trotsky in a retort to Lenin in 1904, before he joined the Bolsheviks in implementing those methods (until they exiled and assassinated him)

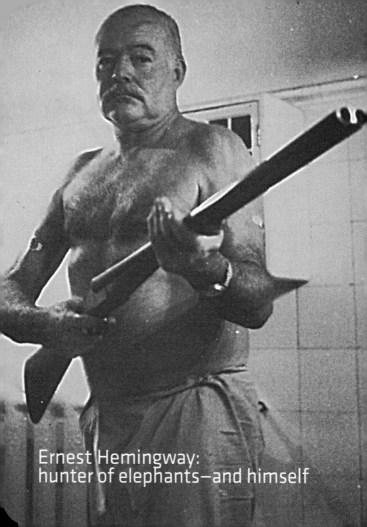

Ernest Hemingway:
hunter of elephants—and himself

Suicide – Before canceling the whole world, why not try changing a thing or two?

Supererogation – The act of going above and beyond the call of duty, performing deeds that are praiseworthy but not obligatory. Christians have debated about this for centuries: how can something be morally right without being a duty? On the other hand, for anarchists who consider no conduct to be compulsory, it might be that all goodness is *supererogatory*—that there is only abundance, both of wickedness and of virtue.

Sustainable Development – Wait, you're talking about sustaining *development?*

Sustainable Technology – One can also sustain injuries—at least up to a point

Sword of Damocles – The thinker Plato, better known for his doctrine that the ideas of philosophers are more real than the experiences of the masses (*see The Republic*), made only one attempt to realize his vision of a philosopher king who would rule with perfect wisdom. As no one would hire him for the job, he had to settle for advising the notorious tyrant Dionysius, a venture that ended disastrously.

The story goes that when another of Dionysius's flatterers exclaimed how fortunate he was to be such a powerful man, the sovereign offered to trade places with him for a day. Damocles eagerly accepted, and Dionysius ordered that he be seated on a lavish couch, surrounded by gold and jewels and waited upon by the fairest boys in the realm. Damocles luxuriated in the attention, shouting out instructions and gorging himself on delicacies until his eyes rolled back in ecstasy. Only then did he behold the sword suspended over his neck by a single horsehair.

At least this is how Damocles' story reaches our ears through Cicero, a typically literal-minded Roman. Had Kafka been the one to pass it on, Damocles might have descried the sword in the eyes of his servants and sycophants. Precarity isn't just for the poor.

Subcultural – A slur conflating lack of cultural clout with marginality and insignificance. White middle-class liberal customs, for example, are the idiosyncratic province of a select minority, no less so than punk, hobo, or trucker customs; but because every billboard and sitcom bustles with idealized portrayals of middle-class characters, many accept that middle-class norms are normal while others are sub-normal. In fact, every subsection of a given culture is a subculture, just as every variant of English is a dialect, just as Puerto Rican immigrants don't have any more of an accent than the white newscasters on prime time television do. Designating any one cultural group as the mainstream, or denigrating another as peripheral, is not just chauvinistic but arbitrary.

Suburban Utility Vehicle (SUV) – A gated community on wheels (*see Property Destruction*)

Symptom – Once we had characteristics; now, thanks to medical science and psychiatry, we have symptoms

Symptomatic Treatment – The perpetuation of injustice and misery by the adjustment of their superficial aspects; e.g., therapy, antidepressants, dieting, charity, career counseling, getting more education, going "back to the land," consumer politics, electoral politics

Systematic – Every individual and situation is unique, but it can be useful to look for common threads. Consistently refusing to do so may indicate that one is avoiding coming to terms with an inconvenient state of affairs, such as oppression at the hands of bloodthirsty tyrants. Without an analysis of the dynamics that give rise to such situations, it can be hard to keep oneself out of them (*see The Forest for the Trees—or don't, as the case may be*).

Some, upon hearing a critique of the social role of police officers and politicians, protest that it may apply to most of them, but they know some who are really good people: "Sure, we have to abolish governments and all that, but here in [liberal oasis] there are such nice folks on the town council! I feel we should treat them with respect, even if that means calling everything off."

This brings to mind the story of the man who, tormented by fleas, managed to catch one between his fingers. He scrutinized it for a long time before placing it back at the spot on his neck where had he caught it, to the shock of his companions. His friends, confounded, inquired why on earth he would do such a thing. "That wasn't the one that was biting me," he explained.

Target Market – A redundancy

Tautology – A statement of which one might say, in the vernacular, "It is what it is"

Tear Gas – In times like these, it takes a lot to cry

Technology – The material manifestation of social relations (*see Apparatus, Reification*).

Technological development isn't inherently linear; we can't affirm or reject it as if it were a single monolith. Rather, there are *different* technologies, which are supplanted as often as they are improved, leaving sedimentary layers of paths not taken. No one today understands the technologies by which the inhabitants of the rainforests of modern-day Brazil related to their natural environment before the first European colonists arrived. We can't recreate the technologies that produced the pyramids of ancient Egypt, nor could they have been built without the social forms that gave rise to them. Who remembers how to use magic lanterns to put on a proper phantasmagoria? Who recalls that the first effort to build an underground public transit system in New York utilized enormous pneumatic tubes?

And human capabilities shift along with technologies. What reader of e-books could memorize an epic poem like the bards of Chaucer's day? Watch a movie from your childhood that struck you with the persuasiveness of its special effects, and see if you're still capable of suspending your disbelief now that you're used to the latest cinematic innovations! Some of the first silent movies were subtitled so the audience could sing along to accompanying live music. Can you imagine a contemporary movie theater audience possessed of the ability to *sing together* spontaneously? It seems that the more life our technology takes on, the less lively we become.

Terrorist – One who uses violence to intimidate, often for political purposes (e.g., police officers and heads of state, and all who aspire to replace them); contrarily, in their usage, a civilian brazen enough to defend herself or others from such violence

Sticks and stones may break their bones,
but words will never hurt them

The – The definite article, singular and definitive, with which nouns purport to represent entire categories or phenomena. Contrary to grammar, nothing is unitary—everything contains multitudes within multitudes.

Theorization – Sure, it's important to refine our hypotheses and learn from past mistakes—but if every worker has to read Hegel to be qualified to fight for liberation, call off the revolution!

Theory – The thing about theory and practice is—in theory, they're the same; in practice, they're different

Thing – A monotonous event

Things are in the saddle, and ride humanity.

– Ralph Waldo Emerson

Today – Tomorrow never comes

Top-Down – Denoting a system in which actions are initiated at the top of a hierarchy. One might think the opposite to be "bottom-up," but this still assumes an "up"; many grass-roots initiatives make this error, attempting to exert leverage through political channels rather than developing the power to achieve their goals autonomously. Better simply to topple pyramids than to attempt to defy gravity.

Totalitarianism – Ideology incarnated as a society; "the Word made flesh," to appropriate Catholic lingo. After the great leader's death, walls throughout the nascent Soviet Union were painted to read *"Even now, Lenin is more alive than the living."* The implications could not have been wasted on the beleaguered workers for whom the boundless possibilities of revolution had been replaced with the inert prescriptions of the dead.

Trauma – "And how do you deal with trauma?"

"Trauma?" answered the Greek anarchist, almost blinking. "We have no trauma."

"But surely, with all that conflict, you must have developed some means of processing the emotional effects. I mean, even here, people are dealing with tremendous trauma, and our demonstrations are tame by comparison."

There is only one time that is important—*now!* It is the most important because it is the only time when we have any power.

– Leo Tolstoy,
The Three Questions

"No, there is no trauma in Greece." The other Greek nodded gravely. "We always say, the struggle is the *cure* for trauma."

The NGO employees exchanged a pitying glance. *How sad,* thought the one who had asked the question. *They're so traumatized, they've lost touch with their pain.*

It's because they're so macho, even the women, the other conveyed with a slight raise of her eyebrow. *They can't acknowledge any vulnerability.*

Years later, having become disillusioned with nonprofit work, she found herself in Thessaloníki, participating in riots and street-fighting against police. Indeed, this was more frightening than anything she had experienced in the United States, but the Greeks did not seem to be more traumatized than her companions in the Bay Area—if anything, they seemed to be better adjusted.

"What do you make of that?" she asked her old friend, when she finally returned home. "I'm not sure what to think."

"That's interesting," mused her former coworker. "They say trauma results from not being able to respond physically; the impact is blunted if you can run away or fight back. And if everyone in the community is participating, that means they can process the effects together without seeing it as treatment. The worst part of being on the receiving end of repression in this country is that it's so isolating. You're supposed to keep it to yourself; you feel ashamed. Even if you bring it up, you just get blank stares."

As social conflict intensifies, abandoning rebels to suffer repression on their own only creates an ever more traumatizing society. There's no way to sidestep the fight; we confront it head on together, or suffer it individually. Struggle is the cure for trauma.

Trial – A formal proceeding designed to emphasize the innocence of judges and lawyers by contrasting them with a defendant, often drawn from the most desperate sectors of society. If this exercise is not sufficient, the defendant is subjected to such an affliction that the worthy jurists can at least congratulate themselves on not being in his shoes.

Tritagonist – The person who is third in importance, after the protagonist and deuteragonist, in ancient Greek drama. Perhaps this word should come back into circulation for use in modern polyamory drama.

Trotskyism – Stalinism would be fine if only it were more international

Trotskyist – Being the most Trotsky, e.g. "Ralph is Trotsky, Noam is Trotskier, but Howard is the Trotskyist of us all."

This spirit of competition has doomed those who would march under the emblem of Trotsky to perennial splintering. As larks gather in *exaltations* and crows move in *murders,* one Trotskyist constitutes a split, two a party, and three an "International"—especially if one of them lives in a different town than the others.

Trouble – Our ancestors were afraid of getting hurt; today, we're afraid of getting "in trouble"

Trust – A principle that can serve all the functions fulfilled by *authority* without any of the drawbacks, since it is conferred voluntarily and keeps power in the hands of those who invest it rather than those who receive it

Twit – A silly or foolish person (*see Twitter*)

Typeface – An alphabet in a straitjacket

Uhtceara – The Old English technical term for the sadness one feels in the hour before dawn

Umpire – Baseball's answer to the police officer—hence the timeless refrain, "Kill the umpire!"

Uncertainty – When an equation balances, where commitments are irreversible, wherever there is mas-

tery, control, certainty, the revolutionary is doomed. In an utterly dominated world, in which causality itself appears to have been pressed into service, all foreseeable conclusions are dead ends; it is necessary above all to create situations that are unpredictable, so as to open up the horizons once again.

Underdog – Set forth like David against Goliath and your foes will think you know something they don't

Unsuitable – High praise

Utopia – A tool for the education of desire. To promote gratuitous consumption, advertisements present a utopia in which grinning idiots find their deepest yearnings fulfilled by household appliances and acne medication. It is disingenuous for critics based in consumer society to accuse anarchists of being utopian—when anarchists speak of a world based on individual liberty and mutual aid, they are simply fostering *other* desires, in order to enable other activities.

The real significance of a utopia is the activities it enables its adherents to participate in. Utopias take on flesh as the social currents they mobilize and steer. The purpose of a vision of the future is to anchor and orient you in the present.

Vanguard – In communist usage, a party that leads from the rear; lest anyone get the wrong idea, they sometimes show their courage by putting themselves at the forefront of charges *backwards*. In early anarchist usage, a group that does not lead, generally doing so from prison, though the word is out of favor.

Veganism – Take a bite out of crime

Veneration – Jeremy Bentham, reformist and utilitarian, began his writing career in 1776 by attacking the authors of the Declaration of Independence as criminals who deserved the full brunt of a military invasion. He went on to formulate the *felicific calculus,* an algorithm intended to measure pleasure and pain; to support animal rights, while defending vivisection as worthwhile suffering inflicted on inferior animals; and to advocate guaranteed full employment in a strictly rationalized economy.

Bentham is best known for his *panopticon,* an architectural design intended to make prisons and workplaces more efficient. The panopticon is a circular building in which all the rooms open inward on a courtyard, so as to be viewed from a central observation tower. The inmates cannot see what goes on in the tower, but they know they may be under observation from it at any given moment, so they eventually internalize this surveillance and control.* This exemplifies Bentham's Enlightenment-era values: a combination of rationalism, individualization, and innovation intended to make people better *discipline themselves.*

Bentham anticipated that future generations would wish to celebrate him for his gifts to humanity. Accordingly, he willed for his remains to be preserved after his death, so that his disciples could meet annually to commemorate him in the presence of his mummified corpse. The University College of London humored this eccentric wish, displaying his remains in a case in the main building of the college and carrying them into the College Council meetings on the 100th and 150th anniversaries of the founding of the school, at which his corpse was listed as "present but not voting."

The mummification process left Bentham's head grotesquely shriveled, with the desiccated skin pulled thin over his skull; consequently, his remains were given a wax head fitted with his hair, and his real head was stored separately. In 1975, students from King's College London stole the head and demanded

* In the panopticon, power sees without looking, while the observed look without seeing. As Michel Foucault put it in *Discipline and Punish*, the inmate of the panopticon "assumes responsibility for the constraints of power; he makes them play spontaneously upon himself; he inscribes in himself the power relation in which he simultaneously plays both roles; he becomes the principle of his own subjection."

a ransom for it; legend has it that in another incident, it was used for football practice in the campus quad. At the opening of the 21st century, after the head had been safely locked away to protect it against further student shenanigans, it turned out that beetles had infested the rest of Bentham's remains.

Though they aspire to hallowed immortality, the most merciful fate that could befall the improvers of mankind would be to be wiped from the slate of history altogether (*see Ozymandias*).

Venture Capital – In this society, capital appears to be the subject of history, acting upon human beings as if we were objects: it determines where we go and what we do, it even gets to have adventures, all at our expense

Vicarious – Typical or characteristic of a vicar: e.g., "vicarious pleasure"

Victim – There is no more compelling justification for violence and oppression than the need to defend or avenge innocent victims—be they the flower of white womanhood, or the casualties of café bombings. All who see themselves as defenders of the defenseless would do well to interrogate their motivations in this light. This goes double for environmentalists and animal liberationists—the advantage of fighting on behalf of those who do not speak your language is that you can act in their name without ever having to consult them.

Vigilante – An attorney at large

Violence – Max Weber defined the state as "a compulsory political organization with a centralized government maintaining a monopoly on the legitimate use of force within a given territory." In this context, "violence" is understood as *illegitimate use of force*: anything that interrupts or escapes the control of the authorities.

Hence, being compelled to pay rent isn't violence, but defending yourself when the sheriff comes to evict you is violence. Pouring carcinogens into a river isn't violence, but disabling the factory that produces them is violence. Imprisoning people isn't violence, but pulling people free from officers who are trying to arrest them is violence.

Conversely, defining people or actions as violent is a way of excluding them from legitimate discourse and justifying the use of force against them. It's often possible to anticipate exactly how aggressively the police will treat a demonstration by how violent the previous night's news reports describe the demonstrators to be. In this regard, pundits and even rival organizers can participate in *policing* alongside the

Though lines of police on horses, and with dogs, charged the main street outside the police station to push rioters back, there were significant pockets of violence which they could not reach.

– The New York Times, on the UK riots of August 2011

police, determining who is a legitimate target by the way they frame the narrative.

In January 2012, on the one-year anniversary of the uprising that overthrew President Mubarak, the Egyptian military lifted the Emergency Laws that had prevailed under his rule—lifted them, that is, except in "thug-related cases." Because the popular upheaval of 2011 had drawn in so many participants and shifted the discourse of legitimacy, it forced the authorities to legitimize previously unacceptable forms of resistance, with Obama characterizing as "non-violent" an uprising in which thousands had fought police and burned down police stations. In order to re-legitimize the legal apparatus of the dictatorship, it was necessary to create a new distinction between violent "thugs" and the rest of the population. Yet the substance of this distinction was never spelled out; in practice, "thug" was simply the word for a person targeted by the Emergency Laws. From the perspective of the authorities, ideally *the infliction of violence itself* would suffice to brand its victims as violent—i.e., as legitimate targets.

So when a broad enough part of the population engages in resistance, the authorities have to redefine it as nonviolent, even if it would previously have been considered violent. Otherwise, the dichotomy between violence and legitimacy might erode—and without that dichotomy, it would be much harder to

The individuals who linked arms and actively resisted, that in itself is an act of violence . . . linking arms in a human chain when ordered to step aside is not a nonviolent protest.

– UC police captain Margo Bennett, quoted in *The San Francisco Chronicle* in November 2011, justifying the use of force against students at the University of California at Berkeley

Never in history has violence been initiated by the oppressed. How could they be the initiators, if they themselves are the result of violence? There would be no oppressed had there been no prior situation of violence to establish their subjugation.

– Paolo Freire, *Pedagogy of the Oppressed*

justify the use of force against those who threaten the status quo. By the same token, the more ground is ceded in what the authorities are able to define as violent, the more they will sweep into that category, and the greater risk everyone will face.

One consequence of the past several decades of self-described nonviolent civil disobedience is that some people regard merely raising one's voice as violent; this makes it possible to portray those who take even the most tentative steps to protect themselves against police violence as violent thugs.

Vogue – Nowadays, you can become old-fashioned overnight

Vote – Those who renounce self-determination in favor of democracy are granted the consolation prize of having a say, usually nominal, in which rules or rulers govern them.

The drawbacks of attempting to access your agency through the Rube Goldberg machine of electoral democracy are plain enough. But this does not explain the intense animosity with which many anarchists regard voting—which does not, by itself, preclude more direct applications of agency, so long as the results are not regarded as inherently legitimate. An anarchist might take a few minutes to vote for the less competent of two evils in a presidential election, for example, without ceasing to struggle to overthrow the government. When it comes to revolutionary strategy, voter abstention is a paltry substitute for generalized insurrection.

So why this fixation? Apart from the dangerous superstitions associated with it, could voting *itself* be hazardous?

One has to dig deep to find evidence of this; yet history is deep indeed, and rewards every researcher with a pet hypothesis. One theory about the untimely death of Edgar Allen Poe—who expired shortly after turning up in poor condition in Baltimore in October 1849—suggests that the renowned author was *voted to death*.

In those days, political gangs would rig elections by shanghaiing vulnerable gentlemen and liquoring them up to make them agreeable. On election day, these unfortunates would be frog-marched around to all the polling stations; once one circuit was completed, their handlers would change their clothes, trim their mustaches, and run them around again. The faster the pace they kept, the more votes they were worth, so it must have been a grueling experience. Nowadays, political gangs accomplish the same thing with advertising and voting machine fraud, but it wasn't always so easy.

Poe was known for his stylish dressing, but when he was found—drunk, delirious, and in the process of dying of exhaustion, at a bar that served as a polling station—he was wearing a cheap, ill-fitting suit that didn't seem to belong to him. It was an election day. So there you have it: voting, horror of democratic horrors, killed the greatest horror writer of all time—and might kill you, too, if you put too much stock in it.

Wage – The exploited are paid minute by minute, so not a cent is wasted on them (*see Salary*); of course, the most exploited are rarely paid at all (*see Domestic Labor, Child Rearing, Community Service, Prison-Industrial Complex*)

We – Mark Twain famously opined that the only people who should use the word "we" are editors and people with tapeworms, but to our knowledge no one has yet undertaken a serious analysis of the power dynamics hidden within this single syllable. "We" sounds so egalitarian, so communal and participatory, when more often than not it refers to unspeakably hierarchical and constraining social configurations. Fascism, let us remember, is also a form of collectivity.

In our preliminary research, we have already discovered several variants of "we," though this is hardly an exhaustive list:

THE LEADER'S WE: "... and we will give our lives, if need be, to defend our homeland!"

THE EXECUTIVE'S WE: "We've got productivity up 25% this year, and we're going to see a real return on that in profits."

THE BOSS'S WE: "We need to mop this whole kitchen in the next half hour."

THE BABYSITTER'S WE: "Are we a little testy tonight? Maybe it's time for us to get ready for bed?"

THE SPORTS FAN'S WE: "We're going to the World Series this year!" Sure you are!

THE ACTIVIST'S WE: "Whose streets? Our streets!" Whose, precisely?

THE PARTY FAITHFUL WE: "Now that the factories are in the hands of the workers, we can commence building the paradise on earth Mankind deserves!" [shortly before a one-way trip to Siberia]

ZAMYATIN'S *WE*: An underrated novel that offered much of the inspiration for George Orwell's *1984*.

Some forms of We refer to entirely mythical social bodies: the patriot's We, for example, thoughtlessly includes everyone who happens to have citizenship in the nation, even if some of them consider themselves enemies of the state. Other forms, such as the We of identity politics, seek to create self-conscious social bodies by premising a mythical common essence on the basis of circumstantial evidence.

Many different forms of collective process are hidden within the first person plural. In the field of the arts, these range from plagiarism—in which two or more parties are involved, but a single one makes the decisions without any regard for the others' desires—to corporate journalism, which is practically no different! In politics, these include the democratic We—"We voted to kick out 40% of our membership"—and the consensus-based We: "We took four weeks to compose a paragraph I could have written in three minutes!"

No discussion of the word could be complete without an examination of the propagandist's We. This is a distant relative of the "royal" We,* in that

* The idea behind the royal We—the *pluralis majestatis*—is that a monarch or other high official always speaks for his or her people. Josef Stalin referred to his dictatorship as the rule of the proletariat, just as the Tsars who preceded him purported to embody Russia. In the same way, the decisions of a Town Council are referred to as those of "the" Town, rather than of the *government* of that town: for example, "For years, the Town of Attleboro has endeavored to prevent residents from gathering downtown on Halloween night."

it's not a We at all. The propagandist's We is most popular among radicals who lack the social skills to collaborate with anyone, yet wish to sound as if they single-handedly constitute a coherent popular movement. A diligent genealogist might trace its history from the mission statements of Bakunin's imaginary secret societies through the "FC" of the Unabomber Manifesto right up to the worst contemporary radical yellow journalism. At best, this We is wishful thinking; at worst, it is the We of the would-be despot, who fantasizes about fielding an army of automations because he cannot imagine any other kind of relationship.

Given all this ambiguity, what proper use remains for the word "We"? We (there it is, "we"!) would like to remind the reader of the old joke in which Tonto and the Lone Ranger are set upon by a bloodthirsty horde of so-called Indians:

"Looks like we're in trouble, old pal," the Lone Ranger observes.

To which Tonto replies: "What do you mean *we*," white man?"

Weather – The primary subject of conversation for those who don't dare trust one another. Populations cringing under dictatorial rule are swept by discussions of the weather as if by a hurricane.

Western – A genre in which the savages are subdued, the frontier is tamed, and the good guys always win

White – Participating in an alliance of convenience that splits the interests of the oppressed (*see Whitelisted, Blacklisted*); counterrevolutionary or reactionary, as in the forces that attempted to suppress the Russian and Ukrainian revolutions; the color that remains when everything that came before has been erased.*

White Ally – The liberal desperately wants to be a *good* white person—to get his hands clean, pay his debts, and move on with his life. He may be prepared to go to great lengths to do so, even accepting the leadership of people of color. But it's impossible to be an ally to *all* people of color at once, as if that designated a monolithic block; Barack Obama does not have the same interests as the undocumented immigrants imprisoned under his presidency. The liberal risks throwing his weight behind the more powerful or privileged in conflicts between people of color—for example, supporting the leadership against the rank-and-file, simply because the former are more visible and more willing to direct aspiring *white allies.*

* Conversely, physicists maintain that white is the color that contains all colors, a sentiment liberal assimilationists are too polite to voice.

Those whose real agenda is to wash their hands are bound to be erratic comrades. Like it or not, there's no sidestepping the complexities of choosing whom to side with and when to stand aside. One cannot make such decisions honestly unless one is invested in the struggle for liberation for one's own reasons—a collective struggle informed by a wide range of perspectives, without leaders or led.

As long as whiteness exists, there's no good way to be white. There is only the fight against white supremacy.

White Collar Crime – A redundancy: clean collar, dirty hands

White Guilt – That much is obvious

White Lie – A harmless or trivial lie (*see Genocide*)

White Noise – Country and western

White Trash – What is processed in the waste treatment center in the black neighborhood; alternately, white people so poor that it's possible to tell how racist they are

Windows – In case of emergency, break glass

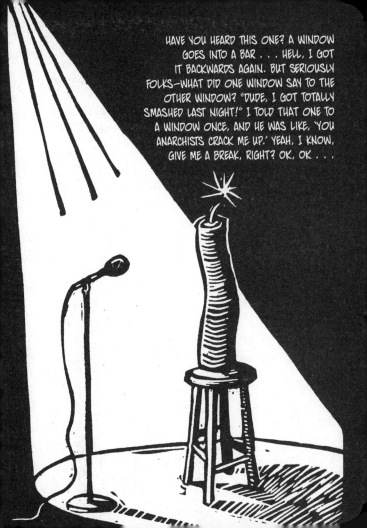

Wishful Thinking – Better wishful action!

Work – The curse of the drinking classes (that's a Wilde idea!); the meaningless routines the capitalist economy imposes on its participants, obscuring the limitless potential of their own self-directed activity (*see Capitalism, Economics, Market*)

Writer's Block –

Y'all – In the southern United States, as well as African-American communities throughout North America, a contraction indicating the second person plural. With the exception of certain blue-collar Pennsylvanians ("yinz") and New Yorkers ("youse"), no equivalent exists in the northern US. This is considered a sign of refinement, but it may simply be that the concept of collectivity is lost on Northerners and wealthy white people.

Youth – Lack of experience in the art of misspending one's life—hence the preponderance of young people in resistance and liberation struggles. If youth is wasted on the young, think how it would be squandered on the old!

Zionism – Between 1881 and 1906, sardonist Ambrose Bierce published an irregular column under the title "The Devil's Dictionary"—a sort of antecedent to this book, though Bierce would doubtless have considered his work inferior. Bierce, who had quipped that "War is God's way of teaching Americans geography," disappeared without a trace while traveling to observe the Mexican revolution.

What does this have to do with Zionism? In one installment of his column, written well over a century ago, Bierce offered the following definition:

> **Manna,** *n*. A food miraculously given to the Israelites in the wilderness. When it was no longer supplied to them they settled down and tilled the soil, fertilizing it, as a rule, with the bodies of the original occupants.

Alas, how history repeats itself.

Zodiac – Above the paving stones, the stars

Colophon – From the Greek *kolophōn,* meaning summit or finishing touch. The colophon is the space in which designers are punished for completing their work by being called to account for their decisions. In this case, to match the character of the text, we aimed for a design rooted in the classical forms, but decidedly modern—a fusion of one of the oldest categories of books with a devil-may-care disregard for convention.

We selected Cala as the text typeface due to its own hybrid nature, derived from historical Venetian Renaissance types and recreated with contemporary touches and without legacy idiosyncrasies. Made by Dieter Hofrichter in Munich in 2011, Cala is a quiet design, one that does not call attention to itself while still being quite beautiful upon close examination. Its **meaty and contrasty bold** and unusually extensive ligatures (fy!) add an essential element of playfulness to match that of the text itself.

Also a hybrid—combining two usually opposing sans-serif influences, humanist and geometric—Klavika is the perfect complimentary display typeface, brazenly modern with its unadorned simplicity. It was designed by Eric Olson in Golden Valley, Minnesota in 2004; he spent years preparing for its creation by touring the world playing hardcore punk music in the band Poison Idea, finally creating a font that can truly fill an otherwise bare page without a hint of pretense.

CrimethInc. bullet, cross-section (according to our critics)

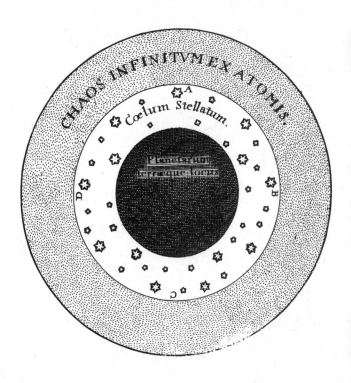

CrimethInc. bullet, cross-section (in actuality)

I'm very much afraid I didn't mean anything but nonsense! Still, you know, words mean more than we mean to express when we use them: so a whole book ought to mean a great deal more than a writer meant.

– Lewis Carroll